LOONEY TOMBS:

Confessions of a Small Town Funeral Director's Son

by

DAVID GOULET

Published by

 GENERAL STORE
PUBLISHING HOUSE

Box 28, 1694 Burnstown Road,
Burnstown, Ontario, Canada K0J 1G0
Telephone (613) 432-7697 or 1-800-465-6072

ISBN 1-894263-13-8
Printed and bound in Canada

Copyright 1999

Layout and Design by Derek McEwen
Printing by Custom Printers of Renfrew Ltd.
General Store Publishing House
Burnstown, Ontario, Canada

Due to the emotional nature of funeral work, most of the names in this book have been changed to protect the privacy of the bereaved families.

No part of this book may be reproduced, stored in a retrieval system or transmitted in any form or by any means, without the prior written permission of the publisher or, in case of photocopying or other reprographic copying, a licence from CANCOPY (Canadian Copyright Licensing Agency), 6 Adelaide Street East, Suite 900, Toronto, Ontario, M5C 1H6.

Canadian Cataloguing in Publication Data

Goulet, David, 1966-
    Looney tombs : confession of a small town funeral director's son

ISBN 1-894263-13-8

    1. Goulet, David, 1966-. 2. Undertakers and undertaking–Ontario–Biography. I. Title.

RA622.7.G68A3 1999   363.7'5'092   C99-901465-X

DEDICATION

*To my family with whom I have shared
the journey.*

Willie & Garry,

This is not a cookbook!

[signature]

PREFACE
It's A Wonderful Life

"Have you ever slept in a coffin?"

Not many kids go through life having to answer that question. I grew up in a funeral home, so that question, and many more like it, were standard fare for me. I am the son of a funeral director. I was born into an unusual home, in an equally unusual town—Barry's Bay.

This book is about the hidden side of the funeral business and my experiences with the mystery of death. Like me, it is also a reflection of the raw character that permeates our little niche of the globe, the Madawaska Valley. This is partly due to the wilderness that surrounds us and the isolation we face. Of course we have highways and roads cutting through the region, but it is an area that most travellers by-pass. Unless you are a cottager, you don't have much reason to visit the Valley. Our small towns and villages still have the feel of the frontier. Life and death seem less complex. There is a remarkable variety of personalities and experiences; a hodgepodge of ethnic groups whose forefathers immigrated to Canada in the 1800s, many Poles, German and Irish.

Growing up I met many old-timers who spoke only Polish, or Irishmen who still preferred clover to maple leaves. The strong Catholic background of both groups was strictly pre-Vatican II. Almost pre-Vatican I. No room for banjo pickin', guitar strummin' priest here. You got fire and brimstone with your sermon, and a side order of eternal damnation. A tour around the back roads of the Valley is like going back in time; to stone fences, old log barns and huge crucifixes at the crossroads.

In high school, I had classmates who would go on to be priests, scientists, engineers, graphic artists, butchers, truck drivers and ditch diggers. It was a mixed bag. This added spice to life. There was often a recklessness to our lives. At one party you might end up discussing the nature of God and the universe all night; at another you'd be cursing your lungs out watching a hockey game. At one outdoor party, we gathered around a pit and watched old lumber burn. When the lumber ran out, the guys threw in an old picnic table. When that was done, they threw in a ten-speed bike. The owner discovered too late it was his.

There was a time when I didn't want to be associated with the image of the country hick. I have lived around different types of people over the years, from stodgy academics to raving megalomaniacs. I don't think I mind being considered a hick anymore, because I've learned that most of the people in this world are "hicks," just simple folk trying to get by in life. It's being OK with who you are, where you come from and where you're headed.

I've learned a lot about life and death because of my upbringing. My parents instilled in me a respect for the dead and those who mourn them. I wouldn't say I've turned out wiser than anyone else. Perhaps I do see things clearer at times. I still have a lot to learn.

I feel fortunate to have experienced the things I have, and sharing them with you is my way of passing on the lessons learned.

TABLE OF CONTENTS

	Preface	v
1.	Earliest Memories	1
2.	Just Your Average Family	5
3.	Making "Ends" Meet	17
4.	My First Time	25
5.	The X Files	31
6.	Keeping a Straight Face	45
7.	The Many Faces of Death	57
8.	The Knights of Jabba	69
9.	Some Days Are Heavier	75
10.	Moving On	81
11.	The Last Farewell	89

CHAPTER ONE

Earliest Memories

RIGHT FROM the beginning, my younger brother Paul and I could sense that our family lived in a special house. For starters, it was newer and larger than most of our relatives' homes. It was a two-story block of a house, with an enormous basement. The odd thing was that we only got to inhabit one third of this "mansion," the upstairs floor. With two bedrooms, a bathroom, kitchen, dining room and a sitting room squeezed into a few hundred square feet, it could get pretty crowded up there, especially when you added a piano, coffee tables and a dog.

Our basement was equally as crowded. There was a "smoking room" with an old-fashioned bottled pop cooler and coffee machine; next to it was a casket showroom; this led to a general storage area packed with boxes of Christmas decorations, cases of embalming fluid and styrofoam cups. At the far end of that room was a large panel door on rollers that opened into a dank concrete section which housed our hydraulic lift. Not too many kids could boast about having an elevator in their basement. It was used to load caskets from the garage into

2 Earliest Memories

the basement showroom, and occasionally as an amusement ride for Paul and myself.

Sandwiched between the congestion of the basement and upstairs, was the ground floor—the parlour itself. Here there were two large rooms, an oasis of space in our sardine-can home. These were the carpeted viewing rooms, and couches and chairs lined the walls. Each had a large metal dais to place caskets on. One room had pink lamps over the dais. It had a dimmer switch that Paul and I would fool with. We would turn it to the lowest setting, like the first hint of sun on a summer morning; then we'd crank it to laser intensity, changing the room into a glaring pink supernova.

The rest of the ground floor was taken up by an office and two washrooms, none of which was much bigger than a phone booth. Not forgetting, of course, the hub of any funeral home—the embalming room. This was a small, white, tiled room with fluorescent lights. It had a large porcelain table along one wall, next to a deep porcelain sink. A cupboard housed all sorts of surgical tools, as well as bottles of chemicals and makeup. The room was kept extremely clean.

Attached to the house were two garage bays. One rarely had a vehicle in it and was mostly used for storage. A massive plywood sheet covered the hole where the casket elevator came up. In the other bay, the big black hearse was parked.

Outside we had a few cedar bushes, some trees and a selection of tombstones on display. They helped dress up our otherwise drab, cube brick home. Farther back of our house were old CN railroad tracks, lots of bush, and a nice hill for tobogganing.

Paul and I had free run of the house, most of the time. There were two exceptions. The first was that if Dad was working, we were not allowed in the embalming room. The second was that when a wake was on, the ground floor and basement were "off limits." It took us a while to understand what a wake was.

People would always be coming to our downstairs, dressed in their church clothes and looking like they wanted to cry. Sometimes we would hear women crying really loudly and we wondered why. Mom and Dad would explain to us that those people had lost a family member; that the person had died and gone to heaven, but their earthly body was still here and our family's job was to help get it ready for burial. The friends and family needed a place to come and say goodbye to their loved one. So for two or three days, the dead person would stay downstairs. The friends and relatives would gather in our parlour to pray and talk, remembering the life of the person who had died. After the brief stay at our place, my dad would drive the dead person to the church in the hearse for a funeral service and burial. In all of Barry's Bay it was only our family that had this important job and that's why the people had to come to our house.

I felt very proud that my family was doing this unique work and that we were the only ones in town with dead bodies in their house; even if I had yet to see one. As we grew older, Paul and I were allowed to come downstairs when a wake was on, but only between visitation hours.

That was my first "contact" with the dead. I would be looking for Mom downstairs, she'd be vacuuming, dusting or setting up flowers. At the end of the room, amid the roses, chrysanthemums and lilies would rest the deceased, dressed all spiffy and lying in a shiny casket under the pink lights. Curious, I would walk over and look closely at the corpse. I'd notice the makeup on the skin and how the hands didn't quite clasp each other naturally. I could smell the flowers and a sweet perfume, but not the kind you'd buy if you were alive.

Most of the dead people were very old, and when you're seven yourself that's just about everybody else. The fact that I was standing next to a dead person never frightened me. It wasn't a real person anyway, just a shell of flesh. If anything I imagined the person's spirit looking down from heaven and both of us viewing this left-behind cocoon.

CHAPTER TWO

Just Your Average Family

Despite my parents' odd occupation, we were no Addams Family. My brother and I grew up in as normal a home as anyone else, albeit with a few idiosyncrasies. Under the circumstances, one would have to expect a few adjustments to domestic life. Let's face it, there's a big difference between living above a funeral parlour as opposed to an ice-cream parlour.

What you learn very quickly is that you are "on call" twenty-four hours a day, seven days a week. Whoever wrote *Death Takes a Holiday* was a liar as far as I was concerned, and since the Reaper never rested, neither did we. When the call came in from the police or the hospital or the family themselves, my dad was off with the hearse to begin the funeral process.

Imagine your family holidays being continually punctuated by funerals. Thanksgiving Day, Easter, Labour Day, and long weekends often were busy times for my folks. The worst was Christmas. Here's the ultimate family holiday; parents playing with their kids and their newly-discovered toys, tobogganing in the fresh snow and then topping it off with a big turkey dinner. We had those things, too. Only many times we had to squeeze them in between body removals and wakes. It wasn't easy having to share in a family's sorrow either, at a time of year when you wanted *"joyeux Noel."* But that's the business and you just had to accept it. We certainly had our share of accepting to do, because Christmas is one of the busiest dying seasons of the year. The elderly in particular tend to just up and die during the twelve days of Christmas. Some say it's because they are lonely and Christmas reminds them of how alone they are and how many friends and family have passed on ahead of them. Maybe it has something to do with not believing in Santa Claus. Whatever the reason, we rarely had a Christmas to ourselves and that sometimes took some of the sparkle out of the tinsel.

Summer was little better. We had a cottage on Lake Clear, a beautiful lake forty-five minutes from Barry's Bay. My dad's family owned a large piece of property there and every year the clan congregated for the summer holidays. We would pack up the car, eager for some swimming, fishing and lazing around with our older cousins. Then that rotten phone would ring and Dad would have to go pick up a body and Mom would have to get ready for the wake. "Sorry boys, maybe next weekend."

The phone became the hub of our life. When it rang, we assumed it was a funeral call, especially if they asked for "Mr. Goulet." When the phone rang during the night, I'd hear my dad get up to answer it and automatically knew we'd have a wake coming. The worst part of it was knowing it was a funeral call and then wondering who had died. Would it be someone I knew? A relative? A friend? Someone important in town or well known? It was a morbid guessing game until I'd hear my dad tell my mom, "Mr. O'Donnell died." Then I'd fall back to sleep comforted in the knowledge it was some eighty-year-old widower who had died and not someone I really knew.

When my folks did finally retire from the business, Mom said the thing she most looked forward to, was not being a slave to that phone any more. I knew what she meant. It meant being able to make plans for a weekend or holiday and not have that phone, a.k.a. the sword of Damocles, dangling over our heads. It also meant when the phone rang you didn't have to brace yourself for bad news. Some people miss the routine of their job when they retire. My parents certainly didn't miss their "routine."

There was one other thing that characterised our funeral home life—silence. Or the need for it, anyway. When grieving people are reflecting on the life and death of a loved one, the last thing they need is the distraction caused by two little boys, pretending they're Mad Dog Vachon and Ray "the Crippler" Stevens, wrestling on their parents' bed. If I had a dollar for every time my mom came upstairs to tell us to "settle down, there's a wake on," I'd be buying drinks for Donald Trump at the Sands in Vegas right now.

We had to keep our voices down: "don't yell so loud," "don't play so loud," "don't put the TV volume up so loud," "don't laugh so loud" and "stop breathing so loud." If we had friends over we had to remind them to not be so loud. One of our most common household sayings became, "Shhhh, there's a wake on." People have often commented on how quiet my brother and I tend to be. It comes as no surprise to us, we were raised in a decibelly-challenged home. The reflex to drop the volume stayed with me long after I left home for university. My two fun-loving roommates could get extremely rambunctious watching hockey games or WWF wrestling. With every "Shoot the friggin' puck!" or "Body slam him, Andre!" I'd instinctively cringe. "Shhh, there's a wake on."

My brother had it worse than I did, I guess. During his high school days he was right into the heavy metal scene. He had saved his hard-earned cash from pumping gas and squeegying bugs off car windshields at Sylvie's Esso to buy a high-performance stereo with Paradigm speakers. AC/DC and Iron Maiden never sounded better or louder. But where's the fun in having an amp that can rattle your windows if you can never raise the volume past three? More than once he tried to sneak the level to three and a half, before my mom would inform him that Sister Rosalyn downstairs didn't appreciate having to say the Rosary to the sounds of Ozzy Osbourne. What's a headbanger to do? At least the need for silence was something we all had to abide by. It was a shared family penance.

Paul and I contributed to the smooth running of our funeral home in various small ways. When caskets arrived, Dad would get the two of us to lend a hand unloading them into the basement showrooms. With our special elevator, we lowered the big metal and wood caskets into the "dungeon." If you were lucky you got to work the elevator controls. All this meant was that you got to stand there and either pull on the left cord or the right one, depending on which way you were sending the elevator. It also meant you didn't have to do any heavy lifting or risk getting a finger severed.

This was a hypothetical accident that was unlikely ever to happen, like putting an eye out with a pea-shooter. When we'd back the caskets, on wheeled dollies, into the showroom we had to go through a few narrow doors and around tight corners. The eye of the needle. Sometimes the casket would come close to jamming on the sides of the iron door frame. Given the expense of the caskets, and the ease with which they could get scratched, Dad would often say, "Better to jam the fingers than scratch the casket." Over the years we never lost a finger or even a fingernail. But I did give up my dream of becoming a concert pianist early on, just hedging my bets.

Understandably, many of our friends and schoolmates were curious about the funeral home.
We got the usual, "Do you ever sleep in the coffins?" to which I would answer, "Only in the summer, because it's cooler."

"Can you breathe in the coffins?"

"Only through your nose or your air runs out."

"Really! Aren't you afraid you might suffocate?"

"Of course not, we set our alarm clocks to go off early."

They'd nod their heads, confused, but hoping to figure it out later. Other times they'd repeat jokes they probably heard from their parents: "I hear Goulet's are having a lay-away sale." Ha ha.

"Bill Goulet—the last man in town to let you down." Ha ha.

"Did you hear, Goulet's are building a fence around their house, people are just dying to get in." Ha ha.

I should have replied "No, but did you hear the one about the funeral director's son who buried all his schoolmates alive?"

One kid actually asked me if my family ever ate human flesh. How do you answer a brain surgeon like that? I replied, "Only sometimes, if we can't afford any beef. Do you want to come over for sausages tonight?"

Ironically the best gag was one they never caught onto—our family name—Goulet, pronounced either "gu-lette" in English, or "goolay" in French. Either way if you add the "h" to make "Ghoulet" you have a very appropriate play on words. The Ghoul-et Funeral Home. The closest anyone ever came was Goulash, which was fitting in a Polish community. Thank God for small miracles.

Everyone has their own way of dealing with the scariness of the unknown. Despite the stupid jokes and goofball questions, my pals had a sincere curiosity about death. Maybe having classmates who actually "lived" with dead people was like dealing with undercover agents. We had the goods on all the secrets of the netherworld.

It wasn't just schoolmates who had a stereotyped view of the funeral biz. I'll never forget the time my brother and I went to Tony's Barber Shop for a cut. I might have been twelve years old and Paul ten. As Tony was quietly cutting my hair, there were two young guys, mid-twenties, talking as they waited for their turn. They were discussing different people they knew down in

Kitchener, where they had been working. They started talking about how one guy was a funeral director and also an alcoholic. Obviously they had no clue as to who my brother and I were.

The one guy said, "Ya gotta expect that in funeral directors. They have to get drunk to forget what they been doing. Most of them are heavy drinkers. They can't help it." His friend nodded knowingly. It was like these guys had personally interviewed every mortician in the country, and were now passing judgment on their sorry fate.

I was not only embarrassed—I was angry. I wanted to shout at them, "Well, my dad's an undertaker and he isn't a basketcase wino!" But I was young and just felt too awkward to do anything. Just then, a piece of stray hair got stuck in my eye and I teared up. Poor Tony. He had been listening to the whole thing and felt awkward, and embarrassed for Paul and me. He must have thought I was crying because of what these guys had said. He wiped my eye with a towel and said, "Did you see the Leafs game on Saturday? They should have won, don't you think?"

I wonder if, after Paul and I left, Tony told those guys who we were. I hope they left with their size ten Grebs firmly in their mouths.

Now, to balance out this terrible tale of adolescent martyrdom, I should detail the upside of living above a funeral parlour. Imagine being five years old and having a whole downstairs floor to play in, when there are no wakes on, of course. It was our little Romper Room (or Holodeck if you're a Trekkie). When Paul and I were a bit older, my big cousin Glenn would come over and the three of us would play war for hours downstairs. One day we'd be defending the Alamo, sniping at Mexicans hiding behind the tombstones outside. Another day it would be cowboys and Indians, and we'd fire our imaginary six-guns and arrows as we ambushed each other throughout the downstairs and basement. Or maybe we'd be comic superheroes, sweaters tied around our necks like capes, destroying a criminal hideout. It was even better than the real thing: Batman never had time for lunch and his mom's ham and relish sandwiches.

Even in my later years, the funeral home remained the perfect place for war games. My friend Rob and I were into the war-gaming craze one summer. We took our old plastic armymen and taped them to cardboard squares, and set them up strategically around the rooms. Tape measures calculated movement and target distances. A set of dice decided the fates of dozens of miniature soldiers. We created an epic of plastic annihilation. We could even simulate night and day warfare by dimming the pink viewing lights. Maybe it was a bit childish for a couple of high school seniors, but it was a lot of fun.

I don't think any of us ever thought playing in a funeral parlour was inappropriate. It was a big empty room with no parents to bug us or to stare at us and make us feel self-conscious as we fired our baseball-bat Bren guns into the Nazi stormtroopers assailing our fort; or, when we were older, turning the place into a chess-like battlefield. The imagination tends to be more free if there's a bit of privacy.

Yes, living on top of a funeral parlour had its perks. How many kids had a shiny hearse to play in? Paul leaned toward Grand Prix driving more than I did, so he spent more time behind the wheel. The hearse was parked, of course. At seven years old he had trouble reaching the gas pedal. He didn't have trouble with the gear shift. One day we were playing outside, and the hearse was sitting in the driveway. Paul decided to race the Indy 500. He jumped into the hearse. His head was just visible above the dashboard, and I could see his hands on the steering wheel. I can still remember the look on his face as he accidentally put the hearse into neutral. The vehicle slowly began rolling backwards, down our sloped driveway. Paul's eyes were as big as baseballs and his mouth wide open in terror. The hearse gained momentum and rocketed (two mph?) down the incline. It went a good fifty feet and nearly smashed into the steel fence of the oil station next to our house. Luckily there was a set of deep ruts just before the fence and the hearse got hung up on them. Dad had rushed out by then. The hearse hadn't even been scratched, which made Dad happy. He was laughing and not so angry at his little Evel Knievel. It was a few months before Paul sat in the hearse again.

Years later, when Paul got his driver's license, he finally drove the hearse for real. He still had a need for speed though. This led to his getting stopped by the ever-vigilant police around Apsley, on his way back from Peterborough to pick up a body. The officer asked Paul why he was speeding. Paul explained that he was returning to our funeral home with a body in the back. The officer scanned the inside of the hearse and noted, "I don't think your passenger is in any rush." Law enforcement just can't appreciate the fast-paced world of the undertaker.

Living in a funeral home had another bonus. It gave us a chance to show off our insider funeral knowledge to friends. We knew they had to be curious, so we'd offer them a guided tour. Some would be totally fascinated and were eager to see the various aspects of the mortician's trade. Others, perhaps more predisposed to nightmares, refused to enter certain rooms. When I would do a tour, I'd open the door to the embalming room and say, "I'll just check to make sure no one's on the table." They usually took me seriously, as if I'd actually invite them to view a half-embalmed corpse. I don't think my dad would have appreciated that kind of word-of-mouth advertising.

Often the smell of the preservatives raised my friends' bile levels, thus the embalming room tour tended to be short. A few had trouble just looking at the caskets. That surprised me. The caskets were elegantly displayed and had about as much shock factor as a car lot. Maybe my friends were having mental pictures of "test driving" these one-way chariots.

I always felt proud when I gave these tours of our home. It made me feel unique, like having a backstage pass at a rock concert. It made up for all those times in grade school when I couldn't bring any cool stuff like scalpels, body bags or embalming fluid to show-and-tell.

Admittedly, not everyone finds a funeral home a carnival attraction. It can be a creepy place, especially if you let your imagination run free and deliberately try to scare the daylights out of each other. One of our favourite games was to lure some of our more fun-loving friends and cousins downstairs into the basement, through the casket showroom, deep into the back storeroom. We'd pretend to be looking for skates, an old toy, a cowboy hat, whatever. We would ask the victim to look for the object in the far end of the room. Quickly we'd turn off the lights behind us as we raced out. As the light switches were in very mixed-up spots, sometimes in the adjoining rooms, the poor victim usually had no idea where to look for the switches. Being left in the pitch dark in the bowels of a funeral home was often enough to freak them out. Even if they weren't too scared by the dark and felt they could navigate their way back to the ground floor, they had to cope with one tiny bit of knowledge—we were sitting in the dark waiting for them. The game usually ended with a hearty scream and a good laugh.

We did this once to our best friend Bernie. We were still grade schoolers at the time. Bernie was easily excitable and had a flair for the dramatic. We led him into the backroom, looking for a box of comic books and sprung the trap. He yelled the minute the lights went out. He must have hit every cardboard box in the room as he scrambled back through the casket showroom. He bumped his shin on a casket just as my brother leaped out of the dark and grabbed him, growling like a zombie.

"HOOUU!" yelped Bernie. He raced on through the smoking room, towards the light of the stairwell. As he passed me, hiding behind the pop cooler, I jumped out and howled, "BRRAAUGHH." He screamed and tore up the stairs like the proverbial bat out of hell. Upstairs, feeling much safer in the light, he was laughing and yelling down at us, "You guys are nuts! Hoouu, you got me good." Hey, what are friends for.

When we ran out of fresh victims, my brother and I would turn our tactics on each other. If one of us went down to look for something in the storeroom, you could be sure the other would sneak down behind and spring the trap. Of course, we both knew full well where the switches were on the walls. But if you had to turn on the light you were admitting you were a chicken and you'd be told so. Better to brave the dark than be labeled a scaredycat wimp.

So you would listen for any sign of movement and slowly edge toward the stairs, waiting for that bullet with your name on it. One day, when Paul trapped me in deep, I decided to try a new strategy. I would out-stealth him. It was during the time of the first ninja movies, like Chuck Norris' *Octagon*, and I was going to prove I had the blood of the ninja in my veins. I knew how patient a ninja had to be. To walk silently you must inch ahead painfully slowly. I breathed only through my nose and as soundlessly as possible.

In that cool, damp basement, adrenaline rushing, you can think of only one thing—how much you need to go to the bathroom! But I was determined to outlast my brother. It must have taken nearly half an hour for me to slide through the casket room and reach the door to the smoking room. It was closed and it took another tense minute to turn the knob. I opened it just a sliver. I could see the stairwell and the daylight from the ground floor. This was it. I swung the door open, leaped to the stairs and up. I was laughing and yelling back, "Haa Ha, you can't trap a ninja! You lose, sucker." I was still laughing when I reached the top floor and strolled into the TV room, proud of my martial arts abilities. The smirk on my face turned to a stare of disbelief. There was Paul lying on the couch watching TV.

"What was all that yelling downstairs," he asked so innocently. "Where have you been for the last forty minutes?"

The little twerp hadn't been hiding down there at all. I had just spent the better part of an hour alone in the dark. This humiliating tactic added a new dimension to our ongoing shenanigans—the scare that never comes. Take your pick, killer suspense and a possible heart attack or feeling like an idiot when you find your adversary lounging upstairs with a fat grin. To this day, if I enter a basement I prefer to be the last in line.

You'd think that all these escapades with hearses and embalming rooms would leave my brother and myself with a gothic approach to life. Yet we were as psychologically average as the next guy. Yes, my brother preferred heavy metal music and drew ghouls on his notebooks—but what grade nine student didn't?

I must confess that one of my favourite holidays is Halloween. I believe All Hallows Eve isn't just about handing out candies to cutely-dressed kiddies; it's a night to acknowledge our mortality. There are things out there that scare us, like death, the supernatural . . . the unknown. For me that's the core of Halloween. Nowadays it's just another Hallmark moment, when it should be about scaring ourselves silly.

In high school, I spent hours carving pumpkins for our annual jack-o'-lantern contest. I never won first prize, but everyone said I had the grossest, most disgusting entries. With accolades like that who cares who won first place. I always wanted to turn our house into a first-class haunted house for Halloween, but my parents had a problem with me transforming our respected, dignified parlour into the Gates of Hell.

I guess growing up in the funeral business did leave me with a slight, ever so slight, pre-occupation with the macabre. I did have an extensive collection of horror movie books. I collected a magazine called *Famous Monsters* and could watch monster movies all day. Other grade schoolers idolized hockey players like Mike Bossy or Darryl Sittler. My hero was the Japanese guy who directed Godzilla flicks. Gee, maybe I *was* a bit weird. I mean when I first heard the cliche, "skeletons in your closet," I thought, "Wow, cool!" When the World Wrestling Federation debuted their scary new wrestler, the Undertaker, Paul and I cheered him as if he were family.

I admit that some things that were commonplace for us, might seem morbid to others. In the days before parcel delivery service, cremated remains would often be mailed to our home for delivery to the families. The ashes would come through the regular postal system. I'd be checking the mail and receive the parcel card. Thinking my mail-order comic books had finally arrived, I'd excitedly rush to the counter. The clerk would cart over the heavy box and I'd think, "I didn't order that many comics!" Then I'd realize that it was someone's remains. I would be momentarily disappointed that instead of *Spiderman Comics*, I'd be carrying home Mrs. Kulshinski's ashes. Then I'd cheer up. How many kids got to walk around Barry's Bay with cremated remains? I remember asking Dad what would happen if the post office misplaced a box of remains or if the address was lost. Dad thought for a second, then grinned, "I guess it would end up in the dead letter office!"

I laughed and added, "It would be pretty hard to return to sender (God)." Nothing like getting a dead body in the mail to brighten up the day.

Oddly enough, I later met a woman whose father's remains did get lost in a large urban funeral home. The elderly funeral director had stashed the cremated remains somewhere in the complex, but then he died of a heart attack. Nobody could find the box of ashes in all the clutter. I could identify with that.

All things considered, Paul and I grew up to be mentally balanced individuals. I still like gothic music and monster movies, between episodes of Teletubbies and Hockey Night in Canada. Would the Addams Family watch Don Cherry?

Chapter Three

Making "Ends" Meet

OPERATING A FUNERAL BUSINESS in a rural area is a balancing act, especially financially. You might have a secure market being the only mortician in your town, but you are also limited to a smaller population base from which to draw clients. Generally, rural folk have modest incomes and are conservative by nature with their money.

My dad was quite young when he built our parlour and began his "empire." He knew it wasn't going to be easy or cheap. To run a proper funeral business involves a heavy financial investment. The parlour itself needs to look elegant and dignified. This is achieved with special lighting, soft carpeting and appropriate decor. The embalming room requires a heavy porcelain table and sinks, surgical instruments and chemicals. Dad had the expensive elevator installed in the basement for the caskets, as well as racks to hold them. There was the smoking room with the pop machine and coffee maker, which had to be re-stocked regularly.

A funeral director must dress the part, too. Dad had a good collection of grey suits and overcoats, plus his trademark hats. Dad could look as suave as a Mafia don in his funeral duds. Battleship grey was his colour. Even his hair went grey early.

No funeral is complete without the hearse, a special vehicle one doesn't find too often at the local car dealership. Supply and demand means hearses come with a high sticker price. They don't come in assorted colours either.

Dad had one asset that helped him balance the finances: his ingenuity. Combining our home, upstairs, with the business, downstairs, was a smart first step. Not having two separate buildings simplified things immeasurably. It allowed Dad to spend more time with his young family while still attending to his work; not to mention the savings on property taxes, hydro bills and phones.

Dad's talent for versatility really hit the mark when he designed his own hearse. One of the problems rural funeral directors have is maintaining the right vehicle for the right job. Often this means owning a station wagon for pickups and deliveries, and a traditional hearse strictly for services. On rural back roads, a low-riding hearse is out of its element and can be vulnerable to all sorts of pot-hole mayhem. Hearses are also noticeable by design, which can be a drawback when trying to guard the privacy of a family during a pickup.

The conspicuous nature of the hearse was demonstrated early in my dad's career. He used a traditional hearse for most funeral pickups and deliveries. It was expensive and hard on gas, but it was considered part of the business. One summer, Dad had to drive a deceased cottager's body back to Illinois. Wanting to get there and back as quickly as possible, Dad asked two friends to come along and share the marathon drive. He put an air mattress in the back of the hearse so they could take turns napping and driving. The mattress was right beside the shipping casket. One of the crew was sleeping under a blanket when they stopped for gas in Michigan. The young station attendant was looking through the side windows and must have been preoccupied by the casket and "deceased" on the mattress. He banged the nozzle on the gas cap as he went to fill it up. The noise woke the sleeper on the mattress, who sat up. The startled attendant leaped back and dropped the nozzle on the concrete. As he high-tailed it inside he yelled back, "You can fill it yourself!" This was one of the drawbacks to owning a traditional hearse. Dad wondered if there wasn't a better way to build one.

Inspiration struck him a few years later, while he was selling used cars as a sideline between funeral calls. One day he was in the city, checking out some specials at a big dealership, when he spotted a vehicle he thought was a large hearse. Curious, he took a closer look. It wasn't a hearse, but a black van with customized windows. Dad felt it would have made a very respectable hearse, with just a few adjustments.

The idea of turning a van into a multi-purpose funeral vehicle kept gnawing at Dad. He phoned a dealer rep for GM and asked how much it would cost to take a regular grey van, install side windows and add a few interior modifications. Suprisingly, the customization wasn't very expensive at all. Dad decided to forge ahead and create his own "designer" hearse, replacing his traditional one.

Dad adapted his van/hearse to suit his needs. From the exterior, with the side windows curtained, the grey van was simple and unassuming. It was the interior that had all the bells and whistles. Running along both sides, just under the windows, were flower rails. The flowers from the wake could be lined along both sides of the van, and with the curtains pinned back, the vehicle transformed into a hearse. The floor had rollers, which allowed for easy insertion and removal of the casket.

This carpeted floor could also be lifted up in two halves and hooked to the sides. This enabled the cemetery equipment to be loaded and transported without soiling the carpet. Before the days of sport utility vehicles, this was truly a death utility vehicle.

The best part about the hearse/van was the price. After all the customizing, the van cost about $14,000. A brand new hearse could easily cost $45,000. By having one vehicle to do the job of two, and at a third of the cost of a hearse alone, not only was he cutting his own expenses, Dad was able to pass the savings along to the families.

Dad tried to market the van/hearse to other funeral directors. He generated a lot of interest in the concept. As expected, many rural funeral directors were interested in the hybrid vehicle. From northern Ontario to Newfoundland, Dad had his peers talking about his van/hearse. Even city undertakers were intrigued by the idea. The van was another option they could offer their clients. The price was right.

In the end, Dad's prototype hearse was the only one ever produced and he used it until he retired from the business. Despite all the positive feedback, no other funeral director would take the plunge. Perhaps the main reason was the long-entrenched image of the traditional hearse. For many funeral directors the long, powerful Cadillacs embodied the funeral business—elegance, style and class. There was no question that Dad's hearse was more utilitarian and much more cost effective. It just didn't look as good. One fellow director actually remarked he had gotten into the business simply because he loved driving the big Cadillacs. You just couldn't get the same rush from driving a "van."

A case of style over substance? Perhaps. The funeral business has evolved into one of slick and shine; polished boots and carpets fine. Yet the back roads of many rural towns are still unpaved and washboard-like. There is still a need for tough vehicles to handle the bull work. Dad looks at modern utility vehicles and sees the potential for an even better designer hearse. Today's vans look very sharp and affordable. Maybe some young funeral director up in Kenora will take up the torch.

Dad's luck in having a multi-purpose home and vehicle also carried over to his staff. With all the long driving and heavy lifting, there's no way one man can run a funeral parlour. Some funeral homes have several drivers, embalmers, and directors at their disposal. Dad couldn't afford a big staff like that. But then he didn't really need one, not when he had a real Jack of all trades, Jack Billings. Jack was helping manage his family's hotel, The Balmoral, a Bay landmark, when he began working with Dad. He often had free time in the day, as he specialized in running the bar at night. Dad needed an extra hand or five to run the parlour. His biggest need was for a driver and assistant at church services. Jack was a barrel of a man, enjoyed driving and was a social person. Funeral work gave him some steady work to fall back on when the hotel was quiet.

He proved to be the perfect sidekick. His easygoing manner and down-to-earth personality matched my dad's. Whenever one was feeling low, the other would crack a joke and bring his spirits up.

Jack was from the old school. You did the work, whatever the hour, whatever the day. Dad could call Jack at four a.m. to drive with him to Toronto and pick up a body, and Jack would never complain. Dad was a young undertaker, Jack was the seasoned local lad; together they made a great team. I used to compare them to Johnny Carson and Ed McMahon. Their size and stature certainly paralleled the TV duo. So did their sense of humour.

Over the years Johnny and Ed shared some interesting times. Each would have run-ins with the highway patrol on the 401. Speeding was often the charge. I suspect in the early days a few "driving with open booze" fines were handed out too. For Paul and me, Jack was like an uncle. He'd come over to the house and holler up the stairs, "Is your pa in?" He was the only person I can remember who used the term "pa" (not pronounced "paw" either). It seemed very Irish to me.

He certainly had the Irish wit. He could tell stories that would shame a leprechaun. He could reprimand you and still make you laugh at the same time. One time Paul was parking the hearse in the garage. There were barely a few inches between the hearse and the walls; it was a tight fit. Paul gunned in the van a tad hard, just missing a casket we had stored against the wall. When Paul got out, Jack yelled in, "Judas priest lad, you only missed that #@$! casket by an arse hair!"

Once, Jack was personally involved with a funeral. His uncle had passed away and he was acting as a pallbearer for the service. It had been a miserable, wet day. As they approached the gravesite and placed the casket on the straps of the lowering device, the wall of the grave under Jack's feet caved in. Jack slipped in, his leg dangling under the casket. The other pallbearers and onlookers quickly grabbed Jack and pulled him up. It was an uneasy scene, but Jack was his unruffled self: "Almost two-for-one on this job, Bill," he commented with a grin.

Jack passed away a few years ago. We still miss him. My family has been blessed by the many good people like Jack that we've worked with. From the florists and cleaning ladies, office helpers and drivers, fellow morticians and service assistants, each played a part in helping us provide a necessary service for our community.

It's not an easy business to be in, when you consider your livelihood depends on other people dying. Sometimes we'd go a few weeks with hardly a funeral, but the bills would still come in and mortgage payments would be due. Mom would be getting nervous about the finances and then we'd have four people die in three days. She felt bad for the families, but also relieved to have the income.

It can be an easy business to take advantage of people. You are dealing with families at a very vulnerable moment. Often a bereaved family will compensate for the loss of their loved one by overspending on a lavish funeral. Many a time my dad could have sold an expensive casket or monument to distraught relatives, increasing his profit margin. Dad may not have been the most professional funeral director in Canada, but he was one of the most honest. He never put on the hard sell to a family. In fact, several times he tried to dissuade poorer families from buying the high-ticket items. Dad believed that if you were honest with people, in the long run God paid you back tenfold.

One year, the number of deaths was quite low. A heavy bank debt began to seem a bit heavier. Then, a wealthy widow died after a short illness. She had a good-sized family; most of her adult children were doing well too. Dad knew this might be a chance to push some higher-priced caskets. But that wasn't right, and he knew it. Let the family follow their hearts.

As Dad showed them the various caskets in our display room, he could see they liked the Solid Oak. This wasn't unusual. Dad had noticed how wealthier families preferred the understated, elegant look of the traditional wood caskets. Though generally less expensive, the Solid Oak was fairly dear. The family would probably take this one.

Then the family grouped around a metal casket, a White Primose, so called because it was white, with a light blush and rose interior. This was more expensive than the Oak. Dad wouldn't mind if they chose this one. They kept looking the caskets over and stopped in front of another metal one. Dad's heart skipped a beat—the Solid Copper. The Rolls Royce of caskets. Very expensive. He had never sold one yet. He had even thought about moth-balling it and using the valuable showroom space for a Cherry Red.

Dad pointed out that this was a very expensive casket. When he mentioned that he had never sold one, the family began to nod their heads. This was exactly the unique casket that would do justice to the unique woman that was their mother. They'd take it.

Mom, Paul and I were eating supper when Dad came upstairs with the good news. He had sold the Solid Copper. Not only that, the family had ordered a big tombstone, on which

Dad made a nice commission. Mom couldn't believe it. Now, no one was popping champagne corks or anything like that, but I seem to recall raising my glass of apple juice and proposing a toast to the rich widow.

I think the funeral business is like any other service industry. If you treat people with fairness, sincerity and respect, things will work out just fine.

CHAPTER FOUR

My First Time

As MENTIONED EARLIER, the embalming room was off-limits for much of my childhood. My parents were no doubt concerned about us seeing dead bodies lying naked on a table, blood draining into a sink and Dad sewing up an open chest cavity—it might lead to nightmares. Go figure.

Only rarely, when we had to give my dad a message (like "It's time for supper"), did we kids catch a glimpse of the verboten room. Through a half-open door we could usually see a pair of legs—yellowish and with ugly, gnarled toenails. The fluorescent light and white tile floor and walls gave everything a greenish tinge, not that a corpse needs any help looking green.

The room always smelled of chemicals and embalming fluid, as if someone had mixed a pail of bad vinegar with a gallon of old ladies' perfume (like the kind Mrs. Creshnek wore to Bingo on Sundays).

As we grew older, the door to the room got wider and we gradually saw the entire body being done up. Then one day my dad must have figured I was old enough to be properly introduced to the wonderful world of body preparation. I was twelve years old, but I don't think age was a factor, so much as my dad sensing I was mature enough. He had been thinking about it for awhile and decided that this was as good a day as any.

I was upstairs reading in my room. Dad came up and asked me if I could give him a hand in the embalming room. I was a bit surprised, as Mom was home and she usually helped Dad when we had a wake on. I figured it must be important if he was asking me, so I headed downstairs. By this time the embalming room was old hat for me. I had been in it loads of times and had seen numerous corpses. I had even helped Dad unload the stretcher from the hearse and wheel the body into the room. But this was different. This was going into the trenches.

Dad needed someone to hold up the head of the gentleman on the table so he could sew the scalp back, which had been cut open during the autopsy. I think I wore rubber gloves but maybe not. Dad showed me how to hold the head and he got busy with the needle and thread. I was quite excited to be actually helping with the real work of embalming.

I studied the texture of the dead flesh and looked for the various incisions and stitching my dad had already completed. The man's lips had been glued shut and the eyes too, with plastic eye covers under the lids to maintain their shape. It was amazing to see how much work was involved with preparing a body for a wake.

Dad kept asking me, "Are you OK? Do you feel uncomfortable? If you feel like stopping, just say so." I almost felt bad that I didn't feel nauseous or faint. Wasn't this supposed to be gruesome?

Within a couple of minutes Dad was done with the stitching and he said that was all for now. I went back upstairs. Mom immediately was checking me for any signs of mental trauma or psychosis. No luck. I was still sane (although today there are some who would beg to differ). She told me that I should always remember to wash my hands well after working in the embalming room. When I thought about it, I had just been touching a decomposing corpse and who knows what kind of germs and chemicals I now had on my delicate skin. I used up half a bar of Ivory on my hands before heading to my room.

I lay on my top bunk for a long time thinking about that dead man. I replayed the scene in my mind and how I had felt holding his dead head in my hands. I felt proud of myself; I had worked on a dead body and had not puked or fainted. I could take it. It was a good feeling knowing that this funeral director's son was no delicate daisy. I had faced the "horror of the dead" and passed the test. I was as tough as that guy Quincy on TV.

A few weeks later, still riding my pride in being Mr. Ironstomach, I was quickly humbled by Fate. Dad had gone to Pembroke to deliver a body to the pathologist and Mom was visiting my grannie, when a funeral director from Toronto stopped in to deliver a body. The deceased was an older man who had lived in the city for some time, but was being brought home to be buried in the family plot.

The funeral director needed help unloading the body into the embalming room, and as a member of the Ironstomach fraternity I was the man for the job. We transferred the body and I was sure I was impressing this undertaker with my nonchalance and easy chit-chat. Imagine someone so young being so used to corpses. As he went to his station wagon to get something I was thinking how foolish people "outside the business" were about corpses. Imagine getting unsettled over such a simple thing.

My inflated head was getting bigger by the minute, when my confrere returned with a big bag. As he handed it to me, I saw a rainbow of colours swishing through the clear plastic. I grabbed the heavy bag with two hands and stared at the contents: intestines, lungs, kidneys, bladder, blood and other assorted entrails.

"I guess you can leave it on the table with the body for now," he said. I just stood there mesmerized by what I held in my hands. I had a horrible flash of a thought: I envisioned the bottom of that bag splitting open and all those guts slopping onto my feet. Mr. Cool wasn't so cool now.

Breaking out of my trance I finally replied, "Yeah, I'll just leave them here, that's a good idea," as if I had originally planned to take them upstairs and leave them on the kitchen table.

I wasn't feeling sick or anything, just kind of stunned. The funeral director must have laughed all the way back to Toronto; I would have too if I could have seen the look on my face. Saucer eyes and half open mouth. That incident taught me that I hadn't seen it all yet and that God always has ways of knocking us off our high horses. Yet, I had passed another test. Despite my shock, I hadn't "lost it."

Dad never pushed Paul or me to deepen our knowledge of embalming. We did help out with removing bodies from hospitals or homes; we'd help lift the bodies onto the table or into caskets; we'd even help dress the bodies. But we never directly worked with Dad as he did the embalming. That didn't mean we didn't glean more about the preparation side of the business over the years.

Generally, the initial step would be cleaning the body, unless it had come from a hospital and this had already been done. Next came the setting of the eyes and mouth with glue in the closed position. The major work of embalming the body then began.

Embalming was basically a two-step process. An incision was made to raise a vein and an artery. As embalming fluid was pumped into the artery, it pushed the blood out the vein. Everything drained into the sink and a special septic system. The abdominal cavity was then cut open slightly and a water-vacuum instrument inserted. It drew out the blood, waste and urine from the chest and bowels; after that a powerful disinfectant was pumped in. When the embalming was complete, the incisions were sewn up and the delicate work of makeup and hair styling begun. Because skin shrinks after death, hair often needed to be cut and fingernails trimmed; men often needed to be shaved.

Dressing the body was the next step. First the socks and underwear were slid on. Then the shirt was cut up the middle of its back and each sleeve separately slid over the matching arm. This was done because the body no longer bent easily at the arms or waist and was in a prone position. The pants were pulled on and the suit jacket, also cut up the back, was put on. In the case of a woman, the same procedure was done with a dress.

The body was lifted into the casket; the jacket and shirt, or dress, tucked in. The casket's pillowy interior was then fluffed around the edges. The final touching up was done: the hands clasped and glued together, the head placed at resting position, the hair combed, perhaps a Rosary placed in the hands. The casket was rolled on a trolley into the viewing room, placed on the dais and the soft lights turned on. Flowers were placed around the deceased.

The illusion was complete; the person was resting peacefully.

CHAPTER FIVE

The X Files

LONG BEFORE Agents Mulder and Scully were investigating mutant cockroaches and pesky poltergeists, the Goulets of 23 Stafford St. were encountering things bizarre.

Take the case of "The Bug Man." One summer a local man died in the woods. I think he had been on a solo fishing expedition, hiking to one of the hundreds of small lakes deep inside the bush. He suffered a heart attack and died. However, his body wasn't discovered until several days after. By then, all sorts of insects had found it too. The body was taken first to the pathologist for an autopsy. We would find out later that he had sprayed five full cans of Raid over the corpse, unsuccessfully trying to exterminate all the pests. He neglected to pass along this vital info at the time.

The body was eventually delivered to our house, on a humid day when my dad was out of town. My mom was as usual tidying the embalming room after the delivery. She noticed a bug crawling out from under the sheet covering the body. She squashed the offensive insect with her shoe.

No sooner had the little bug been dispatched to six-legged heaven, than another one skittered out. Whack! that one bit the dust. Mom was curious as to where the insects were coming from so she lifted up the sheet to inspect it. To her horror she saw dozens of bugs on, around, and emanating from, the body.

This was still early in Mom's career as a mortician's wife. She hadn't yet developed a "curtain of indifference" to unsettling sights such as this. Even cleaning out the cat's kitty litter box could make her queasy.

Well, the sight of those bugs, a species she had never seen before, put her into a minor panic. OK, a full-blown, five-alarm panic would be closer to the truth! Here she was all alone, Dad wasn't expected back until late that night, and a colony of filthy scavenger bugs was invading our home. Even her quick hands brandishing the killer shoe would be no match for this horde. She raced upstairs and brought out a big can of Raid. She sprayed every drop of it over the body. It barely slowed the bugs down. Now she was really scared.

Realizing she needed help, she rang up my uncle, who worked as a custodian at our grade school. He drove right over and suggested using Lysol. This also failed to kill the bugs. Then he said Javex bleach should burn the little critters. It didn't. Mom was at wit's end. How was she going to stop this infestation? She checked her cupboard under the sink once more. She found an old bottle of Rawleigh's insect killer. This was an ancient brand name from the days before they banned DDT. It could have been nuclear waste for all my mom cared. Desperate, she said a quick prayer (to which patron saint I have no idea) and poured on the Rawleigh's. Wham! Whatever was in the old stuff did the trick. The bugs died and our home was once again safe from invasion.

While my family generally felt safe and secure in the funeral home, many people don't. No one looks forward to a visit to the local funeral parlour. Some folks would rather be sitting in a dentist's chair awaiting a root canal, than sitting a few feet away from a dead person. It is these poor souls who take it the worst when something unexpected happens.

A relatively common occurrence would be the power going off in the evening. For a few anxious seconds the parlour would be pitch black and suddenly silent—except for a nervous gasp or whispered religious oath. This happened one night when I was helping out downstairs recording Mass offerings. The lights went out and everyone went silent. I had a terrible urge to do one of those maniacal laughs you hear on cheap Halloween commercials. Prudence got the better of me, though.

If sharing the dark with the deceased can freak some folks out, imagine how they fare if the corpse open its eyes. This unfortunately can happen, albeit rarely, if the glue holding the eyelids weakens. To an unsuspecting mourner the resulting stare can be a tad alarming.

There are many side-effects that can be caused by the embalming process. Every mortician takes great care in masking the natural process of decay. This is part of the professional responsibility he carries with the job; creating a dignified, peaceful appearance for the deceased, thus helping ease the shock to the family. But sometimes irregularities can happen. It might be something minor, like fluid leaking from the nose, mouth or ears. The jaw might slacken and reveal the stitching within the mouth. It could be something major, like gases shifting within the body causing an audible moaning sound through the esophagus.

For the wrong person, in the wrong place, at the wrong time, any of these side-effects can cause a serious fright. More than one nervous visitor fainted at our place. It isn't hard to push an already stressed person over the line.

It doesn't help if you live in a traditionally superstitious community either. Our little Madawaska Valley remains firmly rooted in the legends and beliefs of the peoples who settled here—predominantly Polish and Irish. Both are cultures rich in supernatural tales and mythologies that date back centuries.

Being an area of Ontario that is nestled in obscurity, our small villages have retained their ethnicity; there have been three generations since the original immigrants arrived in the late 1800s.

For most of these sons and daughters of the pioneers, being superstitious is second nature. In fact, the small village of Wilno, a few kilometres down the highway from us, is famous for its vampire legends. The Poles had a strong belief in vampires and they brought this belief with them to Canada. A baby born with a caul on its head (residual membrane from the amniotic sac) was said to be cursed and would become a vampire, unless he or she later ate the saved caul. This belief gradually faded and vampirism became less of a threat to these new Canadians.

Sometimes, when farmers would find their cattle dead in the fields, mysteriously drained of blood, they would jokingly claim that the vampires had awakened again. More than likely it was outsiders making blood sausages at the farmers' expense, but vampires made for better conversation.

In the early 70s the *National Enquirer*, that bastion of investigative journalism, got wind of the Wilno vampire tales and sent a reporter to cover it. As can be expected, the reporter was more interested in making the front page than in the truth. Wilno was portrayed as New Transylvania, with undead bloodsuckers roaming the back hills dining on cattle until a human meal presented itself. Decades later the legend lives on; big city journalists make the annual Halloween trek to Wilno's graveyard searching for cheap laughs among the tombstones. Never mind that the residents of Wilno are tired of the notoriety and would just as soon impale the journalists on wooden stakes.

We never had any vampire problems at our house. The bats living in the back shed didn't have the big ears. However, we did have an incident during one wake involving a mystical talisman and two brainwashed daughters. The two women were in their twenties and their father had just passed away. The two girls had recently gotten involved with some kind of pseudo-Christian cult. During the wake they kept talking strangely about their dad and how he needed protection from evil spirits that might attack his soul at the moment of burial.

On the day of the service, my dad was preparing the casket for transport to the church. This was the last chance for the family to view the deceased before my dad sealed the casket. The two women placed a metal talisman in the casket. Their mother promptly removed it. The girls protested and tried to put it back in. Their mother refused, wanting no pagan occult symbol inside her husband's casket. Dad sided with her and tried to close the casket.

At this point the two girls went totally hysterical. They swooned and ranted at the same time. My dad had never seen anything like it. He was afraid they were on drugs and were about to go completely psycho. Finally the mother told my dad to put the talisman back in the casket. As soon as he had done this, the girls calmed right down. They were as docile as lambs after that.

As the funeral entourage left the building, the mother whispered to my dad, "As soon as we get them in the car and you put the casket in your hearse, open it up again and throw that thing in the garbage."

The closest we ever came to calling in the Ghostbusters was the evening we were visited by a poltergeist. The four of us had just finished eating supper and were talking about Dominic Peroskie, who had just been buried that day. He had been one of the those old lads you'd find sitting on the steps at Palubeskie's General Store, imbibing Catawba sherry. These are the guys that add character to any small town. Mom had known the man and had us laughing recalling some of his sobriety-challenged antics.

Suddenly the lamp switched on in the TV room. And the one in the hallway. With a nervous laugh my mom said,

"Dominic, is that you?" I got up and inspected the lamp; it was brighter than usual and hot. Paul said he could smell something burning. In the bathroom the two mirror bulbs were blazing. Small whiffs of smoke were wafting up from the plastic bulb covers. We tried to turn off the lights upstairs but they wouldn't go out.

Dad rushed downstairs. We could smell smouldering plastic from there, too. We also noticed a faint humming noise. Was our house being taken over by Dominic's annoyed spirit? No, our phenomenon had a very logical explanation. A surge of electricity had flowed through the house, jumping switches and circuit breakers. Dad figured this out and had to switch off our main power line to stop the surge.

The hydro guys responded quickly to our call and inspected the house. They told us how lucky we had been. If no one had been at home or if everyone had been asleep, a fire could easily have started. The surge had melted plastic lampshades and even some rubber wire casing. They fixed the problem temporarily, but to fix it permanently they had to erect a pole with a transformer on our front lawn.

There may not have been a ghost, but I know that what happened was no coincidence. I believe God was teaching us a lesson; a reminder that, but for His grace, any of us can end up nursing a bottle of cheap wine on Palubeskie's steps. I'll bet somewhere in heaven Dominic's soul was having the last laugh on us.

I'm not saying every unusual incident at our house was some kind of divine message. Usually, it was just a case of bad timing. Like the winter my dad had picked up a body and left it in the embalming room before heading to Renfrew to pick up a casket. He told my mom about the pickup, but left out one tiny detail. The body was frozen solid—sitting up. The deceased hadn't been found until several days after he went missing. My dad had turned the heat up full blast in the embalming room, trying to the thaw the body out.

You can imagine what happened. Mom was downstairs and thought she had better check on the embalming room and make sure the heater wasn't overheating. After our experience with Dominic's electrical surges, she was paranoid about fires.

She opened the door and switched on the light and there was a dead body sitting ramrod straight on the table. With her heart pumping a thousand or so beats a second, two things flashed through her mind: either the guy wasn't dead after all and had merely been in cryogenic suspension, or she was about to meet her first zombie.

For a very long, surreal moment nobody in that room was moving or breathing. Then my mom, her subconscious piecing all the clues together, realized the body was frozen in this unexpected position. An air of serenity came over her. She calmly checked the body for thawing (still frozen) and made sure the heat was all right (no smoke), and quietly went back upstairs—where she downed two shots of Canadian Club whiskey and continued her vacuuming. Dad got an earful when he got home that night. He was lucky he didn't follow the pathologist's suggestion—to put the body in the family tub. There would have been more than one dead body upstairs had he tried that.

It takes a lot to spook my mom nowadays. A couple of decades of funeral work toughens you. It wasn't always that way. When my folks first moved into our place, Mom was still green and uneasy around bodies. One day my dad had just brought in a body when he had to rush out on an ambulance call. In those early days, Dad wore two hats—mortician and ambulance driver. I suspect this might have made some patients nervous, hoping Dad wouldn't mix up which hat he was wearing that day. Others muttered that my dad was an impatient man, scouting for business like that.

Anyway, Dad had no sooner left for the hospital, when my

mom heard a low moaning coming from downstairs. She bravely went downstairs to check out the noise. Nothing, not a sound. She went back upstairs and again she heard, "whuuuugh, whuuugh." Maybe the person wasn't dead, maybe it was just a coma. No, that wasn't possible.

Starting to catch a good case of the willies, she called the hospital to see if my dad was still there. He was. She told him the problem and he drove over. Again the downstairs was quiet, no moaning. Dad headed back to the hospital and Mom went back upstairs. Within minutes the moaning started again. This time Mom was more annoyed than spooked. She listened and listened, trying to pinpoint the sound's location. Finally she found the source of her unearthly moans. It was a cable running from our TV antenna outside into our converter box inside. The wind was whipping through it in just the right way to create a low resonance. This explained why it couldn't be heard downstairs. Another X Files case closed.

Occasionally the weirdness was to be found in the homes of the deceased themselves. An elderly woman came to see my dad about a pre-arranged funeral. The lady was something of a recluse and lived a solitary life in the bush. She was eccentric but still mentally sharp. She worked out the details of her funeral with Dad and made a special request: "When I'm gone, can you take care of my cats?" Dad was pretty confident he could find homes for her cats, even if he had to put them out on our farm. Assured the cats would be taken care of, she left content.

The woman passed away a few months later in hospital. True to his promise, Dad made his way to the woman's hermitage in the bush to check on her cats. He was in for a surprise. The cats were easy to spot—because they were everywhere. Cats in her decaying house, cats in the sheds, cats in the yard, cats in the bush. There might have been a hundred cats. The house stank of feline urine and the grounds looked like a giant kitty litter box.

The cats were dirty, scrawny and almost feral. There was no way my dad could find owners for so many cats. They were doomed to starve to death or roam the bush wild—and that could lead to serious ecological impact over time. The old woman must have been spending her pension just feeding them.

My dad knew the majority of these poor cats would have to be put down. There was no vet in our area at this time, nor a Society for the Prevention of Cruelty to Animals. It was a tough problem facing my dad, but he had a tougher solution. The next day he came back with his friend Alfie. . . and Alfie's .308 rifle. It was a relatively humane method of extermination, but one requiring a lot of patience. Alfie could only pop one or two cats at a time, before the rest scrambled. Minutes would pass before they'd sneak back and he could take aim again. It took almost three days to clear out the lion's den. Alfie buried the cats on the land, and the survivors scattered throughout the county.

In retrospect, Dad wonders if the old lady knew what fate likely awaited her cats. She had never said "feed my cats" or "look after my cats." She had said, "take care of my cats." Whether she knew or not, the case of the "Cat Lady" was certainly an unpleasant one for my dad. I think he would have preferred one ghost over a hundred flea-bag cats.

I only ever heard one ghost story that actually raised the hair on my neck. It was a sad incident involving a young local man. He suffered from schizophrenia. He died tragically one night when he leaped in front of a transport truck on a lonely stretch of highway just outside of town. It's the kind of death, senseless and brutal, that shakes a small community.

Several weeks after the funeral, a highschool friend came to class on Monday with a scary tale. His uncle from Sudbury had been down for a visit. When he arrived at my friend's house, late Friday night, he complained about the kids fooling around near the highway. He said he'd seen some idiot running across the road naked. "Don't the young guys around here have anything better to do on a Friday night, than get drunk and go mooning cars? That's how accidents happen."

When asked for more details the uncle described the young streaker and approximated where he had seen him. Both the location and description matched that of the tragedy a few weeks before.

The story sent a shiver up my spine. Of course, there was the possibility that my friend was just pulling our leg. If he was, he was weaving a masterpiece. Then again, his uncle might have been the one making it all up. The folks from our area are prone to tall tales. Someone offered another plausible explanation—maybe it was all a stunt. Some joker had stripped and dashed across the road, perhaps several times that night, trying to frighten people and start a first-class ghost rumour. It was in bad taste, but it was working.

That was the only sighting of the spectral streaker. Do I think it was a ghost? At the time I might have entertained the idea. In retrospect, I'd be willing to bet that the only spirit involved with this story came from a half empty bottle and was named Jim Beam.

One eerie story that I know for sure is true, is the one involving my friend, Barry Lorbetskie, and his brush with death. Barry had come up to the Bay, from Ottawa, for Christmas holidays with his parents. He had to head back early on a Sunday to catch the Boston Bruins play the Ottawa Senators. The weather was extremely cold and road conditions were tricky. Any other day Barry might have delayed his return trip to Ottawa, but with his beloved Bruins coming to town, he had too much incentive. In fact, he had just received a Wayne Gretzky rod-hockey set for Christmas and not only had he made one team the Bruins, he had labeled some of the players' jerseys. The starting line was Orr, Esposito, Moog, Bourque, Lorbetskie and one player yet to be named. He loaded the game and other gifts into his Chevy S-10 and primed the engine.

As he was about to leave, his mother reminded him to wear his silver chain with a crucifix. He rarely wore it, but she had polished it for him and it did look pretty snazzy. The drive to Ottawa in the cabbed truck was cautious and uneventful. Reaching Ottawa, Barry stopped in at his friend's house, a season ticket holder, to pick up the game tickets. His friend commented that he liked the silver crucifix.

Barry was running just a bit behind schedule when he drove back up to the Queensway. He still had to pick up his fiancee Cathy, who had spent Christmas with her family. As he went to merge onto the highway, the truck went over a patch of black ice. The vehicle fished-tailed and with the added speed slammed hard against the right rail. This flipped the truck over, as its momentum sent it scraping and sliding for two hundred metres down the highway. As the vehicle careened upside down, sparks flying from the pavement, Barry clutched the crucifix around his neck with both hands and yelled, "Please Lord, not today!"

Finally the truck smacked into the wall again and stopped. Five long seconds later, Barry crawled out of the broken front window. A passing motorist had notified the police, who arrived soon after. Barry was patiently waiting beside the ruins of his truck. The one officer couldn't believe that Barry was standing. He was even more shocked to see that Barry wasn't even scratched! He told Barry that wearing his seatbelt and a lot of luck had saved his life. Barry knew better.

They towed the wreck to a side street, where Barry's brother, Jim, picked him up. They loaded the contents of the truck, gift boxes strewn throughout the cab, into Jim's car and drove to Barry's fiancee's. He still had the tickets and felt fine. They ended up going to the game, missing only the first period.

The next day, as Barry was unpacking his gifts, he pulled out the rod-hockey set. A tiny head rolled out. He checked the game, everything was intact. The little player with "Lorbetskie" printed on his back was as untouched as his real-life counterpart.

Then Barry saw that the little Bruin with no name was missing his head. Was the decapitated hockey player a proxy of some sort? As if God had heard Barry's plea and taken the head of the nameless Bruin instead? Some might say it was all a lucky coincidence, that the crucifix and plastic hockey player are just colourful details remembered after a very harrowing driving accident. But if your life has balanced on a thread and the finger of death has pointed your way, a silver crucifix and a headless hockey player might be details best not forgotten.

I find Barry's near-death experience fascinating. Encounters with death, while never pleasant, have always intrigued me. You do become accustomed to certain aspects of death if you are always surrounded by it. The spooky stuff becomes gradually less spooky. You accordingly develop a different outlook on life. For people involved with this business, death is a part of your everyday life. You become aware of the rhythm of mortality, that death is another stage we must all pass through on our journey. For me, my Catholic faith was strengthened as I was forced to deal with the reality of death on a daily basis.

A few years ago, I realized how comparably different was my outlook on death, when my cousin was killed in a hit-and-run accident. I was living in Toronto at the time with friends. A bunch of us had gotten together to watch some videos when my dad called. He had bad news, my cousin John was dead. Like most people, sudden news of a close relative dying (especially one so young) hits me like a piledriver. Dad gave me the details on the funeral arrangements and I told him I'd certainly be there.

After I hung up I sat for a minute, taking in what I had just heard. Though still shocked, I felt a sense of peace. I knew John, a life-loving young man, was with God now—where we all will be eventually. For the first time, I could appreciate the New Testament verse that tells us not to weep and wail if our loved ones die, for they are with Christ now, enjoying the peace and joy of eternal paradise. This I knew in my heart was where John was, and if it please God, all of us will be one day. We would miss him of course, but we were really only separated by time, time that flows so quickly anyway.

I rejoined my friends in front of the TV. I didn't tell them about the death. It would have ruined the evening and there was not much they could do about it anyway. I was OK with it, so why burden them too? They popped in a video . . . the remake of *Night of the Living Dead*, a horror classic about zombies. This was certainly putting my fortitude to the test. I was more in the mood for something uplifting, like *It's a Wonderful Life* or even *Ghost*. A movie about dead loved ones rising from the grave to eat living flesh was not the most appropriate film for me to be viewing right then.

But it didn't matter. My feelings about John's fate hadn't changed. I watched that zombie flick and never once did it bother me. They were two separate things in my mind. The film was a fantasy, interesting to me in its own way, but it was not the reality of death that I knew. Later, I would think back to that night. How many people would have been able to sit through a gross horror movie, minutes after learning a favourite cousin had died? It drove home to me the fact that I was different than many of my peers; that growing up in the funeral home had given me something special—an outlook on life that included death. For all the spooky atmosphere and unsettling experiences, life at home offered a window into death. Most people see the window ever so briefly, but we saw it all the time. It can't help but give you a clearer perspective on life.

CHAPTER SIX

Keeping a Straight Face

LIKE ANY OCCUPATION, the funeral business has its share of humour. We wouldn't be human if we didn't laugh, even when faced with the unpleasantness of death. There are the professional in-jokes, the pranks on co-workers, and the unavoidable bloopers. It is the very solemnity of the occasion that often creates the unbearable urge to snicker.

My dad can recount many anecdotes that involve goofs and gaffes during funeral services. These little events might not be particularly funny in themselves; but when they happen in a somber atmosphere, in which no one is accustomed to laughing, they become uncomfortably comedic. The most tempting laugh is the one where you're not supposed to.

For instance, the time my dad was officiating at a funeral service for an elderly woman. The chapel was filled with family and friends. The organist was playing a quiet requiem as the pastor waited patiently at the altar, trying not to look too grim. Dad directed the pallbearers as they slowly escorted the casket to the front. As they approached midway, the woman's husband became excited. Most of those in attendance knew that he suffered from Alzheimer's disease. He stared at the casket and sighed, "Here she comes." Then louder, "Here SHE comes!" And as they reached the front he cried, "OHH LORD HERE SHE COMES!"

It made for a dramatic entrance, all right. My dad had to fight to keep a straight face. It was just one of those times when you couldn't help but chuckle, knowing that if you did it would be both unprofessional and uncaring. It's not that my dad thought the poor man's condition was funny, nor the loss of his wife; it was the timing of the whole outburst that made the moment funny.

Dad kept his poker face on, though. The rest of the service went normally. Then, as the pallbearers made the final procession out with the casket, a familiar voice was heard once again. "There she goes." . . . "There SHE goes!" . . . "OH LORD JESUS THERE SHE GOES!"

This time, with his back to the crowd, Dad succumbed to a quick grin. "Yes, there she goes." In his own sincere way, the man had given his wife as fitting an exit as any.

There were other awkward moments that my dad would have to face. An ongoing one, and one that was not funny at the time, was the whiskey priest. He was an older priest who had had a tough life. He was pre-Vatican II and a throwback to the days when priests held incredible power in small communities.

It was well known that he had a drinking problem. More than once he showed up for a funeral Mass "over the limit." Though tipsy, he had no trouble with most of the Mass. When you've said Masses every day for most of your life, you can switch on the autopilot. The problems would start when he had to refer to the deceased by name. Sometimes he would forget the first name, sometimes he'd forget the last name, sometimes both. Sometimes he'd forget if it was a man or a woman in the casket.

Once he was blessing the casket and as he reached the part where he was to mention the person's name, he murmured to my dad, "Bill, who are we burying today?" A painfully embarrassing moment indeed, yet so absurd Dad wanted to laugh. It was a scene out of a cheap Hollywood comedy.

This priest died several years ago. I remember thinking at the time, wouldn't it be poetic justice if they spelled his name wrong on the tombstone.

One time my dad was on the other side of the laughs. It was during his days as an apprentice with a big funeral home in Ottawa. They serviced a large area and occasionally did rural calls. It was on one such call that my dad and the other drivers were in a small town called Wakefield. It was a drizzly spring day. Dad was assisting with the service and was loading equipment into the trunk of one of the limousines before heading to the church.

The limo was low to ground to start with, and the heavy load pushed it down further. When Dad tried to start it, the engine wouldn't turn over. He got out and checked the car. He found that the tailpipe had sunk into the mud. Dad used a windshield scraper to clear the mud out from around the tailpipe, all the time trying to keep his suit clean for the service. Another driver had seen that the limo was having trouble starting and came to help. While my dad was scraping out the mud, the driver tried the ignition again. It started. He gunned the engine and put it in gear.

The tires spun and Dad was instantly covered in mud. His clothes were a mess. Mud dripped off his hat and face. This classic Laurel and Hardy material had the other guys laughing. Dad walked over to the other funeral cars and found a spare shirt. He was able to wipe much of the mud off and hide the rest with an overcoat. The hat he left on the car roof to dry off. There wasn't time to wait, though. They had to get to the church to set up; three spiffy drivers and one mudman. As the one car sped off, Dad remembered his hat . . . too late. It flew off the car roof into the mud. Dad's co-workers talked about his comedy routine for weeks.

People coming to pay their last respects were another source of amusement. My mom spent many a night downstairs during wakes. She would answer the phone, record the Mass requests or take donations for charities. You'd meet all sorts of folks during the wakes. From the old Polish-speaking farmers to eccentric church ladies, it was a kaleidoscope of personalities.

One gruff old-timer used to get very upset when my mom would record his Mass request and have to ask him for his address. "How many wakes have I been to and you still haven't learned my post box number?" he'd complain. As if Mom could remember the addresses of everybody who walked into our parlour. His complaining finally got so bad Mom had to put a special postit note on the wall with his address on it. She would have liked to tatoo it on his forehead.

Forgetting addresses is understandable but Mom would kick herself when she forgot people's names. Some nights there would two wakes on at the same time and she'd be doing non-stop Mass requests and donations. She'd see so many faces she would get all mixed up and forget names she usually could recall immediately.

This happened one busy evening when she forgot the name of the very well known, influential publisher of our town newspaper. Everyone knew Phil by sight, but Mom had total brainlock and had to ask him his first name. There was a line of people behind him, who began chuckling. They assumed my mom was trying to take Phil down a notch. She wasn't and he certainly didn't see any humour in the situation. My mom could remember his brothers' names and half his relatives, but his name was stuck on the tip of her tongue. He finally gave his name, got his receipt and stormed out. Mom didn't know whether to laugh or be embarrassed. She compromised, grinning with flushed cheeks.

Maintaining a professional demeanor when answering our business phone could be a challenge. Some callers' point blank inquries made you want to laugh. Questions ranged from the succinct, "Who's dead?" and "Is der a wake on?" to the oxymoronic "Who's standin'?"

Some callers could be excused because English was a second language. One such chap had recently lost his father, then a week or two later, his brother Tom was killed in a car accident. He rang up Dad and said, "Tommy dead again, yeah." Dad was able to fathom that the man was merely telling him that a) Tom was dead and b) he required Dad's services again. He was just doing it in one abbreviated sentence.

A few callers could be unabashedly nosy, to the point where you almost wanted to laugh at their ignorance. They'd ask if so-and-so was being waked and then ask, "How'd he die? Was it a heart attack?" They might want a rundown on the person's relatives, even asking, "Will her brother Albert be coming up for the funeral from Brampton?" It tried our patience being polite, when you wanted to tell these gossip-hounds, "Mind your own business."

I put Mom's patience to the test once. In my first year of university, I rang her from Kitchener. As a joke, when she answered the phone, I asked, "Who's dead over der?" in a heavy Polish accent. She didn't catch on and politely replied, "Uh, we don't have anyone being waked right now." I couldn't pass up the opportunity so I started ad libbing, " But I heard Maxie Yeskoskie died. Got hit by a tree his brudder was cuttin' down."

"No, we haven't heard anything," replied my mother patiently.

"You sure, dey said it was a heck of a mess. Would dey need to do an autopsy? Probably be a closed casket, eh?"

That was all Mom could stand; "I'm sorry but that's not the kind of thing we discuss on the phone," was the terse reply.

Realizing I'd played the gag long enough, I switched to my real voice, "Well, what if I come over with a bottle of Peppermint Schnapps and we talk some more."

"You little weasel," she replied, laughing. "I thought it was an awfully odd call. You had me fooled. Don't ever do it again!" I did try it again, but Mom was wise to my voice impersonations. She never got caught like that again.

Being in this business actually allowed my mom a chance to exact a measure of revenge on an old grade school prankster. This particular boy had tormented Mom from grade one onward. The brunt of all his practical jokes and teasing, it was a relief to Mom when they finally went their separate ways in high school.

Much later in life, Mom's school "chum" passed away from illness. He was in his forties then, like Mom. The family had his body sent to the crematorium and the remains, ashes in an urn, were delivered to our home. While waiting for the family to come by, Mom looked at the urn and reminisced. All those years of being picked on flooded back. As she held up the urn, the face of the grinning young bully flashed before Mom's eyes. She tightened her grip on the urn and gave it a quick shake. Instantly, her long-held anger and frustration disappeared. With that one gesture of payback came a sort of forgiveness, too. Mom laughed. She felt embarrassed by what she'd done, but she also felt satisfied that she had finally settled an old score.

Having a sense of humour is a plus in any line of work; in the funeral business it helps you survive the most ridiculous situations. A good example: the hour before their grandfather's wake, a family ordered my dad to open the lower portion of the casket—because they suspected the body had no shoes or socks on!

Traditionally, although the deceased is fully clothed, only the top half of the casket is opened for viewing at the wake. It's purely aesthetics; showing the whole body is unnecessary and distracting. For some reason, this particular family was convinced the body was sockless and shoeless. Why? I guess they figured we were stealing the footwear for our own use, or selling it on the black market.

The family demanded to see the whole body. Dad opened up the bottom half and pointed to the nice socks and Hush Puppies. The family nodded their heads and murmured their consent, without so much as an apology. Dad didn't feel insulted—if anything he was amused. What else can you do, when people insinuate that you, a professional funeral director, are robbing the dead of their socks and shoes? You laugh.

I know I did. I got involved with two bizarre situations while helping Dad with bodies. The first was in mid-winter and the area was blanketed with a heavy snowfall. We had gotten a call from the police to do a removal. A man had committed suicide, hanging himself in the bush.

Dad brought my brother and me to help. He also brought along a toboggan. The body wasn't too far from the road; there was a skidoo trail we could follow on foot to get even closer. We did have to trudge through about thirty feet of knee-high snow. The body was resting against a small spruce.

There were five of us now: Paul, Dad, and myself, plus two police officers. We placed the body on the toboggan. Then for some reason, my dad and the cops walked ahead to the skidoo trail. They started chatting, leaving to Paul and me the task of pulling the toboggan out. Even sliding on the firm snow, it took some effort to move that toboggan. Maybe the adults felt it was unbecoming a grown man to be seen pulling a toboggan with a dead body aboard.

Paul and I were sweating pretty good by the time we reached the skidoo trail. Once on the trail it was smooth sailing, so much so, that we picked up some speed on a down slope. The toboggan started to edge toward the side of the trail. There was a gully to the left and I had a sudden mental picture of our toboggan careening down that gully into a pine tree. Our passenger would go airborne like a rag doll and end up face first in the snow, with only his buttocks and snow boots showing. Now that would be funny!

Shaming myself for such a morbid sense of humour, I quickly snapped the toboggan back on course. Dad and his deputy friends finally lent a hand putting the body in the hearse. Curious as to how my brother and I felt after this grisly chore, the one cop asked, "I guess you lads aren't used to tobogganing with dead bodies, eh?"

"No, usually we go snowmobiling with them," I replied with a straight face. He laughed, but he looked at me with eyes that said, "You're kidding, right?" I wanted to add, " Yeah, we used to take them icefishing too, but they talk too loud and scare the fish away." But that's the kind of humour that gets you branded as a weirdo! Little did I know that something like that had happened to my dad several years before.

Dad and Jack had gotten a call from the police to pick up a body, 'way back on Paugh Lake Road. It was mid-winter and the snow was deep that year. The cops asked if Dad could bring out his skidoo, as the deceased was in his home, which was two hundred yards from any plowed road. No problem. Dad drove the skidoo out, while Jack drove the hearse with a stretcher and toboggan inside.

When they reached the remote farmstead it was obvious that the snow would make it impossible to drive in close and carrying the stretcher would take forever. Dad and Jack drove in on the skidoo and placed the body on the toboggan. Dad began towing it toward the hearse. He was driving slowly, especially since it was slightly downhill to the road. The crust on the snow was hard and thick, so the toboggan began gliding over the icy crust. Before Dad knew it, the toboggan was passing him on the right and sliding in front of the skidoo. He had to stop and untangle the lines and start again.

As they reached the road, the toboggan once again slid ahead of the skidoo and hit the road first. The veteran police officer overseeing the removal was grinning. "Quite the race, Bill," he remarked. "How would that read in the paper? . . .

'Dead man on toboggan passes man on skidoo.'" Dad laughed; that was certainly a headline that would make you look twice.

Probably the most incredible incident I was ever party to, happened in my senior year at high school. Another one of our local 'characters' had died. He was a heavy-set man who had long ago lost the battle with the bottle. He had no family and no money. The only clothes he owned were green pants and work shirts. He wore big Greb boots. He died from liver diesease.

With great trouble, Dad and Jack were able to get the body into the hearse, then out again and onto the embalming room table, using the stretcher. After a couple of attempts to embalm the body, Dad had to give up. The man was just too fat. He really was a massive individual. To do the job properly would have taken three times as much work.

My dad had always been a practical man. He knew there'd be no one coming for a wake, as sad as that was. There'd be the problem of finding clothes to fit him anyway. Dad was doing most of the funeral as a charity case. Preparing the body for viewing was simply not necessary.

Dad decided instead to put the corpse in a body bag, inside a modest casket. The only problem was that the casket was slightly higher than the table. Lifting this huge man was going to be awkward and difficult. Dad called me downstairs to help, while Jack phoned a friend to come lend a hand. With four lifters it looked fairly easy.

Dad spread out the big white liner/body bag in the casket. We took up our positions at the head and feet of the body and lifted. It was like moving a giant sandbag. This is why we use the term "dead weight." A dead body is much heavier than a living one because the weight is pulled by gravity to a central spot. With a body, this is the torso and waist, making lifting from the extremities ineffective.

We had to work one end at a time, up onto the casket lip. We had just about gotten him in, when Dad stopped. "Wait, I forgot to put the embalming fluid in." Dad had decided to pour the embalming fluid into the bag both to sterilize and to provide some preservative action.

We pulled the body back onto the table as Dad opened a bottle of fluid. He emptied it into the bag. As we began to put the body back in the casket, the fumes from the fluid started to reach us. It started as a tingling in the nose. Within seconds we all had tears streaming down from our eyes, our noses were running and our throats itched.

Like rioters escaping a tear gas attack, we stumbled out of the embalming room into the garage. A minute or two later we were fine again. But what to do? The embalming room was still a gas chamber and the body was sitting half in, half out of the casket. We had to finish the job.

We rushed back in and worked on the upper half of the body. We almost had him in, when we had to abandon ship again. This time the absurdity of the situation hit us. We sat in the garage laughing, crying and sniffling. This was ridiculous.

We were a stubborn bunch and we went straight back at it. This time we got the body's torso in and had just to swing the big legs over. Our eyes were beginning to burn, but we knew we were close. As we lifted the legs, the deceased passed a substantial volume of gas. That did it. We all tore outside howling. What a sight! Four men, eyes and noses red from irritation, laughing their fool heads off.

It took us a while to straighten up, then Jack cleared his throat and looked into the embalming room. I was waiting for him to say something inspirational, like "Once more dear friends, into the breach!" But Shakespeare wasn't Jack's style. He just winked at us and said, "Well lads, let's git at it."

This time we got the body in. It did pass some more internal gases, but we kept our composure. Dad closed the casket just as we had to head out again for fresh air. We stood there for awhile rehashing our little escapade. We all felt a bit guilty, laughing over such a sorry situation. Like a bunch of hyenas playing with a dead water buffalo.

We weren't intending any disrespect to the deceased. It was just another one of those moments when you are faced with something so absurd that the only sane response is to laugh. I recounted this story to a friend some years later; she was shocked at how callous and jaded we had been. "How could you make light of such a horrible situation? Didn't you have any respect for that poor man?"

I grinned, "Hey, we weren't laughing at him; we were laughing with him." In retrospect, it wasn't the most sensitive response. Maybe if I had said it with a straight face.

CHAPTER SEVEN

The Many Faces of Death

EVERY LIFE IS UNIQUE, so too every death. And just as some lives are extraordinary, so too are some deaths. Over the course of growing up in a funeral home, I witnessed my share of unforgettable passings.

My earliest confrontation with death, where it was someone I knew well, was in grade three. Every weekday morning, my neighbour Tommy and I would walk to school together. On our way, we usually met our friend Kerry. She lived on the other side of our block. The three of us would walk in together, Tommy and I usually razzing her about how stupid girls were.

One afternoon I was playing outside with Tommy when my mom came looking for us. She told us that Kerry had been in an accident and had been taken to the hospital. That's all she said then. Tommy and I innocently assumed the accident wasn't serious. We joked about how she probably would be wearing a cast at school tomorrow and how we could tease her about that. One of us would probably have to carry her books.

When I went in for supper, Mom had bad news. Kerry's accident was fatal; she had been hit by a transport truck. She had been playing on her brother's bike and lost control, rolling right onto the highway as the truck rounded the corner. They took her to the hospital but there was nothing the doctors could do; she had died.

Died! I couldn't believe it. I was old enough to know full well what that meant. Tommy and I had lost our friend forever. No more teasing, no more trading lunches and no more snowball fights on the way home from school in the winter.

I didn't cry. I guess I was already used to death. I remember our teacher having us discuss Kerry's death in class. Some kid had heard that Kerry's face was messed up. The teacher said that Kerry might look different in the casket because the undertaker would have to put a mask on it. This made me very upset, like my dad couldn't make Kerry look OK for a wake. I had seen Kerry in her casket, she did look very different, but my dad had just used a lot of makeup. He didn't put any Halloween mask on her.

"No, there's no mask. My dad didn't use a mask." I exclaimed. The teacher was surprised at my excited outburst. "Ohh, of course, David. I meant that they use makeup like a mask." I felt my dad's professionalism had been questioned.

Our entire school went to the funeral. A few of us had been in the Polish Sea Scouts with Kerry. It was really just a youth group run by a former Sea Scout. But like real Scouts we had learned the special salute. We lined up at the front doors of the church and saluted her casket as it was carried out. We had no uniforms, no badges or scarves. But it was one of the most moving tributes I have ever seen.

Today, I can't remember Kerry's face, or her voice. Time steals precious things from us. What it hasn't stolen is the memory of her death. I'll never forget that first experience with the clarity of death. How it forces you to accept the reality of life—that at any moment, you or someone close to you can cease to be. No returning. No amount of money in the world, nor power, nor all the distractions life can afford us, will change that unappealing fact. It takes the death of someone you really know to drive that home.

My next experience with the suddenness of death happened in grade six. My friend Rob and I were walking to St. John Bosco School. From our part of town there was just one road to school. We had to go down a hill, across a creek and up the other side of the valley. Reaching the downhill part, we noticed a police barricade. The constable standing there told us we'd have to go around the long way.

Wow, this was different. We could see an ambulance and another squad car down past the creek. Cars never used that road, so it couldn't have been an accident. We started meeting other detoured kids and the theories started. "I bet it's a murder. Why else would the cops be there?" "Maybe they found drugs or something." It was all very exciting, like an episode of Starsky and Hutch.

By the time we reached school, our best theory was that the cops had found a dead body. We passed another barricade blocking the school side of the valley. Everyone was talking about what was going on. In every schoolyard there's one kid who somehow has learned inside stuff before everyone else. Marie was our insider. She told us that someone had found the body of Stevie, one of our classmates, in the valley. "No way!" was our response. She insisted it was Stevie's body they'd found. The schoolyard was buzzing in disbelief.

Stevie lived on the backside of town and the kids from there got to school by way of a dirt track through the bush. Most of us glued our eyes to that bush opening, wondering if Marie was right. As it got closer to first bell, we began to believe her.

Then Stevie and his two friends walked out of the bush. What a relief. We rushed up to him, laughing. "Geez, Stevie, we heard you were dead! You look good for a stiff." He looked surprised. "No, I'm still alive. Who said I was dead?" We were filling Stevie in on the latest gossip and Marie's dumb story, when the bell rang. As we filed into school, the principal approached Stevie and took him to his office. He didn't come back to class.

Just before recess our teacher was called into the principal's office. She returned with a sad look. "Class, the police have released the name of the person who was found dead this morning. It was Stevie's dad. You'll have to use the long way home until they finish their investigation." Talk about a stunned silence. Had it been murder after all?

At recess we got more pieces of the story. Stevie's dad had been visiting a buddy and was walking home after midnight. There were no street lights on that stretch between the hills. He stumbled off the road and fell head-long into a ditch, striking a rock. He was dead when they found him. No foul play, just tragic bad luck.

We later came to the realization that Stevie must have known his dad hadn't come home that night. When he got to school and learned of his own reported death, he must have guessed the terrible truth. We felt like total morons, yet how could we have known? What a terrible way to find out your dad is dead, at school in front of a circus of nosy kids. I learned a hard lesson that day; death may be an inevitable part of life, but that doesn't mean we can take voyeuristic amusement from it.

As an altar boy at my church, I often served at funerals. I enjoyed it. It usually meant getting time off from school and a free lunch in the parish hall afterwards. The majority of the funerals were a breeze. The deceased was like 140 years old, so the family wasn't exactly distraught. We were merely wrapping up the last chapter in a nice long book.

There were several altar boys from my parish at our school, and usually Father Jack would request three from the principal. In Catholic grade schools, getting out of class was easy if you were an altar boy. For this one particular funeral I got the nod, along with two boys a grade lower than mine. Gary, Chris and I trotted down to the church, sniffing the air for fresh baked beans, courtesy of the Catholic Womens League.

We got to the sacristy and put on our robes. Father Jack gave us the usual instructions. I knew the funeral was for a younger woman who had died of cancer. I remember saying to Gary, " Might be a tearjerker." But we "veterans" had seen it all.

The funeral Mass was a heavy one. The church was full, which was not very common on a workday morning. The people in the pews were red-eyed and sniffling. Despite our bravado, the three "veterans" could feel the grief. The woman's mother started sobbing near the end, and I could feel my throat tightening.

The toughest part of any funeral Mass is the final procession out, especially if the choir is singing a soul-shaker like "Amazing Grace." On this day, the choir sang like angels; there wasn't a person in the church who didn't feel emotionally exhausted by the end of that recessional hymn. Yet, we three marched forward like soldiers in an honour guard.

Chris was carrying the cross, Gary and I the big candles. We walked ahead down to the gravesite to take up our positions. This was our first chance to talk since the Mass began. Gary sighed heavily, "Boy, that was a tough one."

"Yeah", replied Chris, "they sure had everyone crying at the end."

"Well, she was kind of young. I guess that's to be expected," I added. This critiquing of the people's reactions helped us reassure ourselves that we were islands of strength in a sea of grief. But hey, that was our job.

At the burial site, the three of us stood at the head of the grave facing the crowd. As Fr. Jack and another priest made the final blessings, most of the people cried openly. I noticed the woman's husband standing next to Father Jack. He had been relatively quiet the whole service. Something about his face caught my eye; I had never seen anyone look like that. He was young, but somehow looked very old. He reminded me of how a dog looks when it's in pain or distress and doesn't understand what's happening to it.

The more I watched him, his eyes swollen with tears, the more I felt a heaviness inside my heart. I felt so sorry for this man. Then, after the last prayer, he pulled something from out of his suit pocket. It was a single rose. He began sobbing uncontrollably and placed the rose on the casket, "She was like a rose to me!" I felt like someone had put a bullet through my chest.

The man started shaking with grief, and Father Jack had to steady him and lead him away. The crowd broke into small groups and walked in silence back to the church. Gary was walking next to me, his eyes on the brink of tears. Chris stared at the ground as we trudged back to the sacristy. I was hoping they wouldn't start talking, my throat was so tight I could barely swallow. We weren't so tough now. That moment of clarity had touched us, the moment of heart-wrenching loss.

We regained our composure as we tidied up the altar. Chris was the first to say it: "Well, that's the hardest funeral I've ever done." Amen.

We went downstairs to the hall for our free lunch. People were chatting and a few were smiling or laughing. We too started to joke around, talking about school and hockey. The human spirit has an amazing ability to revitalize itself. The pain was already healing . . . but baked beans have never tasted the same since.

The death of a young person is always devastating. It is the shock of loss in the face of abundance. Youth is the Spring—a time of energy, innocence and hope. Death is the Winter—a time of weariness, darkness and gloom. They are naturally incompatible.

There have been many young deaths in our small region over the years; car wrecks, sudden illness, suicide or accidents.

Each was a shock to the community. There would be two that would shake me badly.

The first occurred while I was a volunteer in Tanzania. It was three years since high school graduation. I was stationed in a remote mission along Lake Victoria. There were no phones. I was on my little motorbike, heading for our main station in the town of Mwanza, when I stopped at one of our neighbour missions for lunch and to pick up any mail that had come in. I lucked out and found three letters and a parcel for me. The package was from Mom, and it had taken four weeks to reach me, but even month-old news is better than nothing.

I sat down in a comfy chair and opened the parcel. Newspaper clippings. I scanned one briefly and saw a headline, "Barry's Bay man dies in canoe accident in B.C." A horrible feeling came over me. My friend Simon had written me just two months earlier, excited about going to B.C. for the summer as part of a survey team looking for gold. But it couldn't have been Simon that died, he was an experienced kayaker and a strong swimmer.

The next clipping had his photo and a similar headline. That moment of terrible clarity was with me again. My friend was dead. I sat there in shock for several minutes, poring over the clippings for details. Simon and the rest of the survey team had been working on a remote glacial lake. They were crossing the lake in a canoe when a storm must have blown in suddenly and capsized them. They were in no danger of drowning, they all wore life jackets. They had died from hypothermia in the frigid water.

Two of the other letters I received were from friends writing about Simon's death. It was a weird sensation knowing that it was already a month since the accident. Everyone else had been at the memorial service; they'd had their chance to grieve and move on with life. I felt like time had raced ahead of me.

I can't remember much else, except riding my motorbike to town in a rage. I was lucky I didn't get killed that day. I wasn't sad: I was angry. Why Simon? He was so full of potential. Of all our gang, he was the adventurer. He loved the outdoors and was always looking for something new to try. Before going to B.C. he talked about going to West Africa as a volunteer. He was searching for a place to share his many talents.

My friend Willy said it best: "With all the jerks in the world, why did God take a nice guy like Simon?" In my heart, I knew Simon was with God now, sharing in that unending love. But taking him this early wasn't fair. He could have done so much with his life —good stuff. How could God allow such waste?

That's the million dollar question, isn't it? Every time a young person dies, we ask that question. The answer seems lame, but is no less true. God allows bad things to happen to good people. It isn't easy to come to terms with that.

I learned a lot from Simon's death. I am not immortal. Simon and his crew had been careless, they had used a canoe instead of a proper dinghy. A typical mistake of youth, assuming nothing bad will happen to you. They had underestimated the risk, like I would have, and had paid the price. Yes, take some risks in life, but not unnecessary ones. Keep in mind that Death looks for every chance to claim us, so don't make his job any easier than it already is.

Simon's death hit me hard because he was a close friend. Another death would occur while I was overseas that would also shake me, though I hardly knew the person. This time I was working in Samoa, in the South Pacific. This mission wasn't as rough as Africa. We even had a phone in our house. Once every couple of months I'd call home.

One Saturday, I rang up Mom. It was summer back in Canada. When Mom picked up the phone I said, "Is dere a wake on?" in my heavy Polish accent. But she had heard the little beep when the long distance signal clicked in and didn't fall for it.

We talked for a bit and then she said, "Oh, and say a prayer for the Bloskies. Their teenage daughter Anne Marie hasn't been home for two days and she's not the type to run away." As soon as my mom said this, I got that horrible feeling again. Intuitively, you know something is very wrong, but you pray it will turn out to be otherwise.

Mom rang me at work early in the week. Very bad news. Anne Marie's body had been found in the bush. She had been raped and murdered. This was unbelievable. A girl murdered by some sexual predator. In Barry's Bay! Sure, our area had its share of manslaughter cases and even a murder or two, years ago. But not like this; not a harmless young girl from a good home. That kind of brutality didn't happen in our area, it was a big city problem. I was stunned.

A couple of weeks later, Mom's parcel with the newspaper clippings arrived. The murder had turned Barry's Bay into a circus. There had been the usual media frenzy, photos of police tape around the grocery store Anne Marie had worked at, and rumours of a lynch mob ready to bring about justice.

The murderer had been found, a teenager. He had fancied Anne Marie and had become obsessed with her. Walking her home from work one evening, he made a pass at her. She rejected him and he couldn't handle it. He got rough with her, she fought back and threatened to tell her parents. He then crossed the line and descended the downward spiral into the blackness that lies deep within each one of us. He murdered her and violated her body. The police found her body partially buried in the bushes.

The boy was an outsider. His family had moved into our town only recently. If there was any consolation, it was knowing it wasn't one of our own that had done this. Mom wrote that Anne Marie's funeral was one of the biggest ever seen in Barry's Bay, and one of the most moving. This beautiful young girl had touched many lives.

The boy's family were equally as devastated. They moved away—how could they stay? In a small community like ours, they would be a constant reminder of that horrible time. They had received threats as well, from a few ignorant locals. Their son had irrevocably changed the destinies of both families. There is only one word for an event like this—senseless.

Though I was a few thousand miles away, I was just as shaken by the tragedy. This was my home town, a place I thought was immune to such violence and darkness. I barely knew Anne Marie, only meeting her briefly at arena dances or at the grocery store. I knew her older brother better. We played touch football and floor hockey together. I mailed him a short note from Samoa, basically encouraging him to pray to Anne Marie for comfort, for I firmly believed she was watching him from heaven. What other advice is there?

With Anne Marie, I realized how much one death can affect a whole community. Our naive little town had lost its innocence and had the tombstone to prove it. The ugliness of violent death, usually reserved for American television, city news shows and faraway places like Bosnia or El Salvador, had visited our simple oasis. Welcome to the real world.

It was a death that time would have difficulty eroding. Such an extraordinary story is hard to forget. One of the few that, for some reason, is larger than the life itself.

Another example of this was the death of our long-standing Member of Provincial Parliament, Paul Yakabuski. Mr. Yakabuski had been the Tory MPP of our riding for umpteen years. He was a consummate politician and a native of Barry's Bay.

In his later years, as most elderly statesmen do, he put his work into cruise control. He still fulfilled his job description, but took more time to smell the roses. He was beginning to suffer health problems, around the same time our riding came under review by the provincial government's amalgamation committee. They were suggesting our riding be merged with another to form a new, larger jurisdiction. The government approved the recommendation and would initiate it when the next election was called.

Mr. Yakabuski's health worsened as rumours of an early election circulated. He was more and more unable to fulfill his duties; he hinted that he would retire from politics and not contest the next election.

On the day the government called for the election, the riding Mr. Yakabuski had represented for decades ceased to exist. It seemed poetic, because Mr. Yakabuski had also just passed away.

Politicians and media gathered at our parish for a stately send-off. The premier also made the trip to pay his respects. The man who would have been his main rival for the newly created riding's seat, Liberal Sean Conway, was also there, he too being a native of Barry's Bay.

I remember thinking how poignant Mr. Yakabuski's death was. His riding died with him. That's as close as anyone has ever come to "taking it with him." It seemed such uncanny timing, like destiny was neatly closing the final chapter of a book.

I noticed other deaths like this. My friend's father was a farmer, a farmer from the old school, where hard work was the only creed. There are many such men in our area. The modern world might call them workaholics, but these men lived to work as much as they worked to live. Summer, with its fifteen hours of daylight, is their idea of heaven.

My friend's father died on such a day, killed when his tractor flipped over while trying to pull a heavy load. He died on the land he had spent so much of his life tending. Everyone commented that it was a tragic loss of a good man, but it was fitting that he died while doing that which he loved. His life was the farm, as was his death.

A few years later another "man of the fields" died while bringing in the hay. He suffered a heart attack from the heavy work and humid weather. His family, acknowledging the life of the man, transported his casket to and from the church on a hay wagon.

In a country setting, you are confronted with unusual deaths that stem from the very environment itself. There are the icefishing fanatics who risk thin ice, just to drop a few lines where no one else dares. Or the hunters who spend more time drinking than checking their targets. There are inexperienced cross-country skiers who get lost in the bush.

Summer brings tourists and cottagers to our lakes and forests. It never fails to produce tragic deaths, like the drowning of a five year old Toronto boy as his parents unloaded groceries into their cottage. Or the summer a honeymooning couple asphyxiated in their cabin after the gas stove leaked. In nearby Algonquin Park a young couple was killed by a crazed bear. Lightning storms struck exposed campers, killing one but sparing another within the same tent. Four-wheelers raced over hills and trails, one flipping on a careless driver.

In a land full of trees, the lumber trade can be lucrative. It can also be a dangerous one for the men that fell the big trees and those that skid and cut them. Falling timber, crushing logs and buzzing saws—it makes for a deadly workplace.

Even driving to a funeral in our area can be dangerous. I know of at least three incidents where someone died in an accident while trying to make it home in time for a loved one's funeral. By coincidence, two of the victims shared a same last name, "Peplinskie," though they were not related and they died years apart. Our local roads wind around lakes, climb up and down hills. Rock cuts and log trucks abound. A distraught relative, usually driving from a distant city, can become careless with disastrous results.

Living in the country doesn't mean there's a better chance you'll die; only that there are more different ways for you to die. They say variety is the spice of life; perhaps in a morbid way it's true of death as well.

Chapter Eight

The Knights of Jabba

No MEMOIR of my teenage years would be complete if I didn't tell the tale of the Knights of Jabba, for it helps demonstrate how growing up in the funeral home affected my sense of humour.

Midway through my final year of high school my friends and I created a fictional fraternity of spiritual explorers called "The Disciples of Jabba." This group would evolve into the "Knights of Jabba" and become the stuff of rural legend.

It began innocently enough with a newspaper article in our local weekly. Four of us, my friends Pat and Bernie, and Paul and I stayed after school one chilly night to build a snow sculpture for our upcoming school winter carnival. We knew no one else was bothering to enter a sculpture, so we figured as long as we put something up there, we'd win. The theme was "Hollywood movies."

We had no idea what to sculpt, so optimistically we began with a large base. As with most ice sculptures, the base is the easiest part and we devoted most of our sweat and snow to it. A couple of hours later we had transformed a snowbank into the Tower of Babel. Now all it needed was an intricate sculpture to adorn it.

We dumped a huge blob of snow on top, then searched inwardly for inspiration. Had we been artistic in any way, we might have recreated a scene from *Gone With The Wind* or *Rocky*. We might have sculpted the likeness of John Wayne, Clint Eastwood or Sylvester Stallone. We settled for Jabba the Hutt from the *Star Wars* movies. By doing the massive worm-like alien, we would save time and energy.

This was simplicity at its most pure. We rounded off the edges of the blob of snow, added a few folds of fat and iced it down. After several hours of shoveling snow and hauling water to make slush, we had a huge dais with a giant maggot to show for our frozen fingers and wet boots—a mound that vaguely looked like Jabba the Hutt. It was a proud moment. To top it off, we carved the name of one of our less beloved teachers, Mr. W., on the dais as a "tribute."

We had first prize in our back pocket. But we wanted more. The accolades of our peers were not enough. We called in the media. Well, he was a reporter anyway. He worked for the local paper and had a sense of humour. He was rushing to cover a hockey game in Palmer Rapids, but stopped by to take a photo. Pressed for time he asked us to write an accompanying article and drop it at his office.

This added a whole new dimension to the scene. We had a chance to put our own slant on this sculpture story. So we did what any group of high school kids would do—we embellished. Our story told of a group of Austrian religious artisans who were visiting Canada and demonstrating the spiritual power of snow sculpting. They had been invited to the high school by one of the teachers, Mr. K., who was well known in the community as a leader in his church. They called themselves the "Disciples of Jabba" and claimed they had mystical connections.

Amazingly, the paper printed the story unedited. They thought it was humorous. The issue hit the stores the next day. At school we were either seen as crazy, incredibly funny or retarded. We couldn't have been happier with the results of our hard, icy work. The teacher mentioned in the article, Mr. K, got a good laugh out of it too.

To carry the gag a bit further, we wrote a followup letter to the editor from the Disciples, mentioning they'd be staying around to witness the upcoming Timberfest (our town's winter carnival) festivities, hoping to continue sharing their magical sculpting.

At this point the real fun was to begin. People in the community, especially outside of the school environment, began talking about this group the "Disciples of Jabba." Some thought it was a real cult. *Star Wars* musn't have been a popular film series around Barry's Bay, because no one made the connection with the films. They began calling Mr. K. for more information. My mom was also hearing rumours circulating, from people at our place for wakes. This was great! We had created something with a life all its own. What power!

We had to keep it going and, if possible, make it bigger. Goaded on by our fifth member, Fly, I put an ad in the paper. Trying to parody the Knights of Colombus, the ad said that the Knights of Jabba were recruiting new members and that initiations would be conducted at midnight, on Friday, at the school. "Bring candles and incense." At the same time, Fly had placed all kinds of posters up at school. It was during school house elections and we had our newest recruit, Hammer, running for Grand Wizard of the school. We also had Mr. K. running for the school's spiritual adviser position again.

We took the hoax to a new level. The occult overtones were accentuated and we took perverse pleasure in creating this fake cult. However, as often happens with the grandiose schemes of teenage smart-alecs, the you-know-what hit the fan. Mr. K. was not amused. What had been innocent fun had become deliberate trouble-making in his opinion. He corralled me in the cafeteria and asked me to step outside. Between calling me names like "idiot" and "blockhead" he berated me for involving the school and himself in this farce. Considering that several parents were concerned about a real cult taking root in the school, he let me know bluntly that my actions had been "boneheaded" and "not the least bit funny anymore." Unfortunately, my friend Pat saw us from a second floor classroom. Not knowing the mood of the "conversation" below, he yelled out the window, "Jabba rules!" This did not help my situation.

After the tongue-lashing, my classmates rallied around me. I had been oppressed by a member of the administration. I was a martyr for the Jabba cause. The Knights of Jabba had become more than an inside joke, we had become anti-establishment outlaws.

I was torn. I knew I had to print a retraction in the paper about the ad. If I didn't, I risked alienating myself from a respected teacher and probably other staff as well. But how could I knuckle under to "the man" and keep the respect of my peers. They'd see it as wimping out.

I was able to solve the dilemma. I wrote a retraction stating that the school had nothing to do with Knights of Jabba. I carefully avoided any hint that the Knights might be a hoax. Thus, I placated the school and Mr. K., while maintaining ample room for the continuance of the Jabba hoax.

It almost backfired. That winter a kid in a lower grade committed suicide. Making it worse, he had been a fan of the Dungeon and Dragons game and listened to heavy metal music. All the fantasy imagery referred to in his suicide note pointed to an occult connection. The media hyped this angle for all it was worth. Once again the Knights of Jabba were being talked about in the town. We kept a low profile for a month or two until the paranoia passed.

Gradually, our little group of Knights began to expand and eventually we had about twelve or fifteen guys actively promoting the Jabba cause. Whatever that was. It was a male-bonding thing. A way for a bunch of guys to raise some good old-fashioned shenanigans, hopefully with a touch of cleverness.

We needed a logo. Fly came up with a good one. It consisted of a crown, representing authority, above a single open eye, representing omniscience. It looked like something you'd see tattooed on a Druid priest or painted on a Masonic lodge's mailbox. It was mystical and very cool.

It would become the centre of a perfect coincidence. Our school musical that year, which most of us Knights got involved with, was Rodgers and Hammerstein's *The King and I*. Someone pointed out the uncanny parallel. Our Knights of Jabba logo was of a crown and eye. The King and I. It just added to the legend we were creating.

Graduation would split up our group, but not diminish our antics. We kept the Knights alive in many ways. One year we raised hell in the local papers that our K of J candidate in the provincial elections was being black-balled by the media. That had some locals scratching their heads. Most summers we'd enter softball tournaments under our Knights of Jabba banner, once even dressing up in white long-johns like Droogs. This angered some of the other teams. Our philosophy was this: in twenty years, which would you remember, who won the tournament, or those nuts playing ball in their underwear?

Three times we entered the Timberfest parade, and won once, carrying Big Joe Mufferaw's giant pipe through town. We sent a fake demo tape in to a heavy metal magazine and got a rave review. We sponsored a woman's netball team in Samoa and had T-shirts made. How mythical did we become in Barry's Bay? Well, when the local paper ran a contest to find an acronym for our town's postal code - K0J 1B0—a kid wrote in "Knights Of Jabba One Big Organization."

In university I made a video documentary on the Knights. I incorporated Valley superstitions, rustic dialogue and cattle being slaughtered. I told my classmates the documentary was a real history of a rural pride group. Some believed me. My professor kept rolling his eyes viewing it, but I still got an "A".

Mom used to hate the mischief we'd get into. "Your father and I have to live in this town. We're trying to run a respectable funeral business," she would moan, reminding me that they might be judged weird by association.

The Knights of Jabba remains a bunch of fun-loving guys, typical of our area. One of our many mottoes is, "Raise hell, while you can still lift the Devil." Wherever there are gullible people and free media, the Knights will be there.

CHAPTER NINE

Some Days Are Heavier

THERE ARE MOMENTS in our lives we refer to as "definitive" moments. These are times when we learn inner truths about ourselves; for example, the day you got married, the day you moved away from home for university or the night you wrecked Dad's car coming home drunk from a party. These moments leave white-hot images burned into our memories. They shape our personalities for years to come.

One such moment occurred for me two years after my high school graduation. I had just finished a preparatory year with a missionary group and was awaiting assignment to Africa. I was home for the summer and enjoying being with friends and family. It was a great summer to be twenty years old.

It was a hot one that year, one of the few summers where we had sunny skies from May until August. Good haying weather too, unfortunately, which meant hard work for some of us. But there were still plenty of days for swimming down at the public beach, throwing the kids from the summer recreation program off the raft and flirting with their counselors.

Our friend Bernie called us up and invited us over for a BBQ. Paul went over to help marinate the meat and sip a pint or two. I was still at home when Dad called. He and Mom had gone down to Eganville for something. "The police just contacted me here in Eganville. Jack's not available and there's a body to be picked up in Palmer. Can you and Paul go?"

I could smell those BBQ'd burgers already, but of course the business comes first. "Yeah, we'll go," I replied, "where's the body?"

"It's at the Anglican Church. It was a suicide. Probably a hanging. The police are waiting for you."

"OK, we'll leave right now."

I rang up Bernie's and told Paul the situation. Fortunately, he was only starting his second Black Label, so could still drive the hearse. It was a gorgeous afternoon, warm but not muggy. It was a pleasant drive to Palmer, the sun was sparkling off the lake as the breeze gently swayed the poplars and pines.

It took about thirty minutes to reach Palmer, and another five to find the church. Two cops were waiting outside with the caretaker. As Paul and I pulled the stretcher out of the hearse, the one cop walked over.

"'Afternoon lads. Your dad's not around, eh?"

"No, he's in Eganville. We'll do the removal," I replied.

"Well, are you prepared?" he asked.

"Yeah, sure," I answered, "we brought the body bags and stuff."

"That's not what I mean," he said, "are you prepared for a mess?"

"Dad said it was a hanging, right?" I asked, wondering what he was getting at.

" No. The guy shot himself with a shotgun . . . in the head. It's a real mess."

Paul and I shrugged our shoulders. "Well, we might as well get it done." We carried the stretcher up the steps into the church sacristy. The police hadn't been exaggerating. It was a mess. The body lay in the centre of the room. The walls and ceiling were crimson splashed; body fragments were lying across half the floor. Our eyes took the whole scene in as we positioned the stretcher beside the body. One of the cops approached me with a bag.

"We'll need the skull and brain fragments for the autopsy. Can you put them in this bag?" and he handed me a clear plastic bag with some rubber gloves. I was a bit surprised that he was asking me to do this. For one thing, I thought it was pretty obvious what the cause of death was. Secondly, if it's evidence then he should be doing it—that's his job.

"Don't you guys handle that?" I asked.

"Nope, that would usually be your dad's job," he replied.

Resigned to the grisly task, I donned the gloves and began picking up the skull fragments. "Any idea who this poor guy is?" I inquired.

"He's a McCormac. But we're not sure which one."

I went to school with the McCormacs. The younger brother was in my grade. I didn't know the older brother as well, but I certainly remembered them both. The body lying there in front of me could be my age, a guy I had graduated with. And I was picking up his remains and putting it into this ziplock bag.

I tried to look at the head and identify him. But it was impossible. "What would you want to do something like this for?" I thought out loud. The cops laughed, nervously. We were all nervous, and yet fascinated at the same time. This was death in its harshest form. It's a strange feeling, getting to see such horror firsthand. You can't help but stare at it. To me, it's not morbid curiosity, so much as a chance to observe human mortality. It is both repulsive and mesmerizing at the same time.

But Paul and I were sons of an undertaker. We were there to do a job and we stayed focused on that. I handed the full bag of evidence to the police and helped Paul lift the body onto the stretcher. We zipped up the body bag and wheeled the stretcher out.

"You lads thinking of inheriting your dad's business some day?" asked the cop.

"Not anymore," I replied.

We talked briefly outside. We found out that the body had been discovered by the cleaning lady. She was next door at a neighbouring house, still shaking and in shock. What a fright indeed.

"Well," sighed the caretaker, "I'd better get to work scrubbing that room. I pray it's the last time I ever have to see something like this." I felt sorry for the poor man. In many ways his job would be the toughest.

Paul and I headed back. We talked about the incident and tried to think which McCormac it must be. We talked to normalize the whole thing. It was just part of the business. We both agreed it was the most graphic thing we'd ever seen. The drive back to the Bay was a time of clarity for me. I was alive, the body in the hearse was not. The colours of the leaves, the sun, the lake all seemed clearer somehow.

When we got home, we headed over to Bernie's, still in time to finish off some burgers. Paul popped open a well-deserved beer. We told the rest of the guys what we'd seen. They were understandably shocked. They asked us how we could do it—how could we work with corpses like that and then come home and eat hamburgers. What answer could we give, we weren't ghouls or anything. Of course it's not a pleasant job, but someone has to do it. It's our family's business. You simply do it because it has to be done.

The next day at lunch, Dad told us he had seen the cops down-town we'd "worked" with. They were impressed with his two sons. They didn't think, when they saw us arrive, that we'd be able to cope with the situation. As it turned out, they felt we had been more at ease than they were. It was like Paul and I had passed a test. Faced with a terrible scenario, we had remained calm and strong.

There's an unfortunate flip side to being so at ease around death. You forget that not everyone has the same perspective as you. You need to respect that fact. I learned this the hard way. The man who had killed himself was not the younger McCormac, my classmate Bob, it was his older brother Brian. I had a chance to see Bob at the wake. I was just getting home after a softball game and Bob was outside talking with relatives.

I walked up to him, in my dirty sweatpants, and blurted out, "Hey, Bob, how's it goin'?" like we were at a high school reunion or had bumped into each other at the post office. He put on a brave face and said, "OK, thanks. How have you been?" I chitchatted a bit and then parted with a cheerful, "Well, see ya around, take it easy."

As I was walking up our inside stairs, I froze about halfway as my brain processed the past two minutes. "How's it goin?. . . Take it easy." What was I thinking! Bob had just lost his brother, horribly. That's the best response I could come up with, "How's it going?" Bob must have thought I was some kind of jaded ice man. Why couldn't I have said, "Sorry about your brother." Or, "My condolences," something that would show I had some compassion.

I was so proud of my indifference to a violent death, I forgot how to care. I felt ashamed of myself. I remembered how Jesus, a guy who would have had the best perspective on death, wept for Lazarus, his friend who had died. He even raised Lazarus back to life. If Jesus, who knew that death was not the end of life, could cry over the loss of a friend—then I could share in my classmate's sorrow.

This epilogue to the whole event taught me an invaluable lesson. Yes, I had learned that I had a stomach for this business, but I also learned that having a heart is much more important. As undertakers, you must consider the living as much as the dead.

CHAPTER TEN

Moving On

MY FASCINATION with death's skeletal hold on us would continue well after I left the confines of Barry's Bay. Youth doesn't end after high school, but it's on the way out. For most kids, heading off to university and college is a sign of passage. You leave the relative safety and security of your tiny community for the bright lights and congested air of the big city. This time it's not for a shopping trip, either. It's a chance to experience freedom and independence. No more parental rules or having to mind your manners in a town where everybody knows you and your family.

For the first time, you can be whoever the hell you want. You have entered the exciting post-secondary campus scene. The first thing you notice is that you have returned to the bottom of the food chain again. Almost everyone is your age or slightly older. The girls are foxier, the guys better built. Everyone just seems so cool. This is your new environment. A fresh country bumpkin, trying to look as cool as the seasoned seniors. You start to think, "Maybe being a big fish in a small barrel wasn't so bad after all." Better than being a sardine in this ocean. Especially when that ocean is full of academics eager to sell you their philosophy of life, based on some outdated fifteenth century writer, or worse, a hip, post-modernist thinker.

Near the end of my freshman year, I became frustrated and bored with university life. I wanted to seek truth in the real world, rather than trying to figure it out from books. I joined a Catholic missionary order as a lay volunteer, heading to Tanzania in East Africa.

Life was hard there. Food was not plentiful and the economy was lousy. The people were tough because of their environment. Pregnant women would often give birth right in the fields as they worked. The resiliency and pluck of the Tanzanians never ceased to impress me.

There were two events in Tanzania that would give me insights into life and death there. The first was my own brush with death. Death by snake bite, to be precise. While I was at the language school, learning Swahili, our night watchman killed a spitting cobra. He shot it with a homemade bow and arrow—Robin Hood had nothing on this guy.

He warned us to keep an eye out, as cobras usually mate and live in pairs. The next night, he spotted the second cobra as it slithered down a drain pipe. I had just finished reading an article about a British biologist who captured snakes for study in Zambia. The article even showed the simple trap he used. Thoroughly inspired, I decided to make my own trap and to capture our second cobra. Using a long metal pipe (diameter about six inches), I constructed the trap. I tied a burlap sack to one end of the pipe; inside, the bag connected to the pipe via a one-way door made from cardboard. The snake was supposed to curiously slither down the pipe, through the one-way door and into the bag—no way back.

I set up the trap next to the drain and blocked all possible exits. The snake, if it was still using the drain, would have to go through the pipe to get out. For three days I religiously checked the bag every morning and evening. Nothing. My classmates, about nine Indian missionary priests, ridiculed me mercilessly. They were used to cobras and said my trap was not going to work. An old Dutch priest said I was wasting my time.

With my ego bruised, I decided to dismantle the trap. I poked at the bag once more, still hoping to have caught the cobra, but it was empty. I pulled off the bag and lifted the other end from the drain opening. Looking down the pipe I noticed a blockage. Possibly mud or something. Then I noticed it move slightly and the light caught the shine of scales. I thought it must be one of the many lizards that roamed the grounds. But it was too big. Finally, a bell went off in my head. The cobra was in the pipe.

With my adrenaline surging, I slowly lowered the pipe and stuck rocks into both ends. Then I ran for help. I got just about everybody in the school. The Indians were skeptical but brought a couple of long iron rods in case. The Dutch priest said that I must be mistaken and wouldn't believe a cobra would sit in a small pipe like that.

I brought a big African hoe, with a sharp steel edge. We lifted the pipe end to force the contents out. Nothing. The Dutchman laughed, "See, there's nothing in there." Some fluid dripped out of the pipe. There had been no rain so it couldn't have been water.

I shouted, "It's spitting venom. Drop the pipe!" As soon as the pipe hit the ground a black rope sprung out. It was indeed a cobra. Instantly it started to raise its head. I launched my hoe right at the head, but the snake was too fast. It ducked back and as I leaned forward, it was in a perfect position either to spit at my eyes or strike my face with its fangs.

A metal rod swooshed past my head and caught the cobra by surprise. The Indian priests, experienced with killing cobras, had acted in the nick of time. Two more rods beat lethally down on the snake. I swung again and took the snake's head off with my hoe.

The snake was almost six feet long, minus the head. With the help of two Polish priests, I skinned it. We were curious to try tasting the flesh (fried first), but since we didn't know how to fillet the meat without ripping the venom sack and potentially poisoning ourselves, we threw the meat to the birds.

I became an instant legend. The school staff started calling me Bwana Nyoka, Lord Snake. Call me lucky. The venom spit from the cobra could have permanently blinded me, or, if the snake had bitten my face, killed me. No wonder Africans have such a fear of snakes. The creatures are scary enough in broad daylight, but imagine trying to evade one at night. I realized how close I had come to death. I shivered with fear. I had never felt like this before. It made me appreciate the thought of dying an old man in a warm bed, peacefully. It's not something we Canadians would think of as a luxury, yet for most of the world it certainly is.

Just having a proper wake and funeral service is something we take for granted. One of my fellow missionaries in Africa, a long-serving German named Brother Goddard, died suddenly from a massive heart attack. We traveled four hours on washboard roads to the mission he had worked in. He had died Thursday morning, we were burying him late Thursday afternoon. There was no time for a wake or long ceremonies. The hot climate and prevalence of flies and disease meant that the dearly departed had to be buried quickly. Decomposition begins immediately. There were no funeral homes, no embalmers, no coolers. There was no safe way to preserve a corpse.

The local parishioners brought flowers and fresh greenery to mask the smell of death and brighten Brother Goddard's simple wooden coffin. After a simple Mass and humble procession to the graveyard, Brother Goddard was laid to rest. One day you walk the earth, the next you're lying in it. Traditionally, Tanzanians mourn their dead for weeks afterwards, as if to compensate for the rapid burial. It is a time of intense emotion.

In one case, our school's cook lost a baby to illness. It was the second baby he and his wife had lost in as many years. The normally shy young cook became distraught and violent. He was convinced it was witchcraft. All the priests at school made a point of attending the funeral service. This show of spiritual force was the only way to persuade him that the evil had been forced out from his home, never to return. The alternative would have been a witch-hunt and certainly someone would have been killed.

Our ancestors could have been just as superstitious. Lack of scientific knowledge and entrenched customary beliefs provided ample room for this. There's not much difference between modern rural Tanzanian funerals and those of our country's pioneers. Hard lives and hard deaths are the common denominator. This brings a certain simplicity to the funeral customs. You live, you die, you are mourned and then the living get back to work.

Climate and financial resources dictate so much of the whole process. As technology advances, our ability to preserve the dead evolves. This in turn changes how we bid them farewell. The ancient Egyptians had very advanced knowledge for preserving the dead, mainly royalty; notice how elaborate their funeral customs became.

There is a good example of how technology has changed the mourning process, in Samoa. I worked in this small South Pacific country for a number of years and it proved a fascinating place. A nation with one foot in antiquity, the other in our modern world.

While in Samoa, I mentioned to a co-worker that my father was a mortician and that I had grown up in the business. My friend suggested I visit Sefo's Funeral Home, which was conveniently located across from the national hospital. I agreed it would be interesting to see how a Samoan funeral home compared with ours.

I wasn't expecting too much. I grabbed a taxi to Sefo's and was fortunate to find both him and his wife Ana at the parlour. I found them a young, jovial couple, always wearing a warm smile. When I told them of my interest in their work, and my similar background, they got very excited and insisted I take the grand tour. Sefo talked as he proudly led me through his business.

I was impressed. Sefo handled about forty funerals a month, a large number comparable to some parlors in major Canadian cities. He employed sixteen people; from the drivers of his four Cadillac hearses and Landcruiser (for rural areas), to his carpenters who built caskets from local hardwood. He had just opened a wreath shop and his crematorium oven was due to arrive by ship.

Sefo explained that Samoan "wakes" could last up to two weeks, sometimes longer. Thanks to the introduction of air conditioning and freezers, a body was often kept fourteen days or so, until all the relatives had paid their respects. Since many of the kin had to fly home from Australia, New Zealand and California, the two-week wake was a necessity.

In order to preserve a corpse, it was usually kept in a large freezer until final viewing. However, when Sefo became the first islander in the region to obtain his embalmer's license (studying in New Zealand) he was able to offer that option. Families with a little extra money could now have their deceased embalmed by Sefo, eliminating the freezer process. The body was simply left shrouded in a cool room, fully dressed and prepared for viewing. The body was not put in the casket until burial day, as Sefo and Ana had to check it daily in case of fluid leaks. Sefo did have a freezer unit for those who chose to forego embalming or for cases where a body was decomposing more swiftly than usual, as in cases of terminal disease.

I thanked Sefo for the tour. He and Ana appreciated my interest in their work. Not many visitors dropped by who could appreciate their business. As I left, Sefo asked me if I might take a Samoan wife while I was here. I replied that I doubted it. He then added, that if I ever changed my mind he could arrange that as well: "I can take care of the living as well as the dead!"

A few months later, when my folks came down to Samoa for a visit, I introduced them to Sefo and Ana. In fact they took my folks out for supper. Sefo was particularly excited when my dad mentioned he had recently put an addition on to our funeral home. Sefo asked my dad to sketch a floor plan of our parlour on a napkin. Dad was surprised at this interest in our house's layout.

Two weeks after my folks left, there was a huge fire in Samoa. Sefo's Funeral Parlour burned down. Luckily they were insured. Hmmm. I have seen Sefo's since they rebuilt it, bigger and better, but I didn't see any obvious resemblance to our funeral home.

Perhaps my best funeral story from the South Pacific comes from the isles of Tuvalu. This speck of a nation consists of nine tiny islands. They are atolls, islands formed from coral growing atop ancient underwater volcanoes. Typically, the highest point is six feet above sea level. Dig a hole and you hit water pretty fast.

In Tuvalu, trying to bury someone "six feet under" is no easy task. This was demonstrated when a middle-aged man died suddenly from heart disease. His name was Walesi and he weighed about four hundred pounds. The family had to bury him that day and it took most of the day to carve a hole out of the coral rock. It took ten men to carry Walesi's coffin to the grave. They placed him in, but there was a slight problem . . . sea water had seeped into the grave as the tide had risen. The casket was actually floating on the water, barely two inches under the ground's surface. The burial crew would either have to wait until late that night for the outgoing tide to lower the water level, or they would have to force the casket down.

There was no way they were going to bury a dead man in the dark. Using their own body weights and heavy stones, they pushed Walesi's casket deeper. Water flowed over the casket and onto the ground around. They got the casket about two feet deeper. Quickly they started shoveling in the coral and sand. It was a comic, if macabre, battle to bury a massive floating cork. It took fourteen men about half an hour to put Walesi to rest. Someone commented that Walesi had always wished to be buried at sea but didn't want the sharks to eat his body. He got the best of both worlds in the end.

The creepiest story I ever heard in Samoa came from my girlfriend's family. A fisherman from her parents' village had been swept out from the reef and was presumed drowned in the waves. Her cousin, a strong swimmer, was asked to help find the body. At low tide, in calm weather, it's possible to walk along the reef edge. The search party saw what they thought was the body, but it was down deep and under a coral ledge. The cousin was asked to swim down and check it out. He dove in and swam into the shadows.

It was indeed the lost fisherman. The undercurrent had him resting under the ledge. The diver had to grab the corpse and pull him to the surface. During the ascent, the gases shifted within the body and the cousin was startled by an underwater groan. It didn't help that the body's eyes stared forward and the mouth was open as if screaming. The search party returned to the village, the cousin visibly shaken.

That story made me appreciate the work of our own police divers who locate drowning victims in our lakes. Those waters are even darker and murkier. To bump into a body lying in a bed of weeds must be unnerving.

Stories about death find fertile ground in my memory. Perhaps most people care to forget such things. I'm fascinated by them. Death is another stage in our existence. It is perhaps the biggest, grandest puzzle left for modern man. If there is one thing each of us on this planet shares, it's mortality. We will all pass through death's gate. That alone should hold our attention. Like the cobra, death can be feared, admired, detested, studied, or even sometimes defeated; but not ignored.

CHAPTER ELEVEN

The Last Farewell

W**HILE I WAS ISLAND HOPPING** in the south seas, my parents began looking to retire from the funeral business. Paul and I had expressed no desire to take up the trade, so Dad decided to sell. It wasn't easy to find a buyer. For one thing the value of our funeral home was quite high. Mom and Dad had built up a strong customer base and we had expanded twice.

The other problem was that we lived on top of the parlour. There were very few veteran morticians interested in living on the business premises. Our funeral home was too expensive for a young undertaker to buy. The funeral business on a whole was changing. There were fewer independently-owned funeral homes and more conglomerates, especially in the cities where funeral homes had become like franchises. Dad was worried he might have to sell to a conglomerate.

But as it often does, providence entered the scene. Dad received a call from a young funeral director interested in our place. His name was Shaun O'Reilly and he was the son of an undertaker. In fact, his father had been the undertaker in Barry's Bay before my dad. He had sold the business to Dad.

Though he wasn't working the trade at the time, Shaun had his funeral director's license and was looking to purchase an independent parlour like ours. The price tag was still a hurdle though. Coincidentally, Dad and his accountant, anticipating the financial obstacles for a buyer, had developed a purchase agreement which involved work "in lieu of" capital. This sort of deal helped buyer as well as seller. Shaun would work for my dad for five years, at the end of which he'd become the owner and my parents would retire. In fact, when this financial arrangement became known, it was used as a model by other small town funeral directors wishing to retire. Dad still had his innovative touch.

Part of the deal was that Shaun and his family would move into the funeral home immediately. This made sense as both Paul and I had moved on and my parents were ready to start phasing out of the business. They didn't move too far away though; in fact my parents bought the house right next door to the funeral home.

The five year transition went well. The partnership with Shaun proved successful, and timely when my dad broke his leg one year. Just a few short years ago my folks officially retired from the business. The sign on the parlour now reads "O'Reilly Funeral Home." Shaun has since made some changes. He bought a traditional hearse and added another garage bay. He has his own style and continues to put his own stamp on the business.

My parents have appreciated retirement. They can make plans to travel or visit relatives, without worrying that they'll have to cancel at the last minute to handle a funeral. The telephone is no longer the messenger of doom. My folks are just two average residents of Barry's Bay now, and loving it. This doesn't mean they look back on the business with regrets. They are both proud to have served the community in their own way. Mom and Dad remain grateful to the hundreds of families who entrusted them with their loved ones, at a very painful time. The business provided a good, steady income which allowed us some small luxuries in life. It wasn't easy work, but no work is easy if you want to do it well.

I hope this book has given you, the reader, a taste of the funeral director's life and an insight or two about death. You and I will be going through that dark door someday, that's the sobering reality of it all.

To order more copies of

LOONEY TOMBS:
Confessions of a Small Town Funeral Director's Son

send $18.95 plus $5.05
to cover GST, shipping and handling to:

GENERAL STORE PUBLISHING HOUSE
Box 28, 1694 Burnstown Road
Burnstown, Ontario, Canada K0J 1G0
Telephone: 1-800-465-6072
Facsimile: (613) 432-7184
URL: http://www.gsph.com

VISA and MASTERCARD accepted